Wild Camping on the Skye Trail

David Crawford

Also by the author

Trekking in Nepal

Author's notes

Hill walking can be dangerous. It should be undertaken only by people with an understanding and acceptance of the risks, and the experience to evaluate them. Nothing in this book removes the need for you to accept responsibility for your own safety and well-being.

I offer recommendations for various products, websites and suppliers in the book. I have no connection with any of these, nor have I received any reward or inducement from them. Those mentioned are ones I personally have found useful. Other products, websites and suppliers are available.

CONTENTS

PROLOGUE

It is my final day on the Skye Trail. I have only 15 more kilometres to go before I reach the finish in Broadford. I am looking forward to a comfortable bed, a hot bath and a well-earned pint after seven days' walking and six nights' camping. The weather is dry, the sky clear and I am feeling in good spirits physically and mentally. What could possibly go wrong?

I round a corner and see five calves, six cows and a large bull blocking my path! I know all the advice about not getting between a cow and her calf, so am wary; but I need to keep going. I slowly approach the herd, and as I do they start to saunter along the path in front of me, stopping to chew grass but always keeping an eye on me and staying a short distance ahead as I approach. I am happy to continue like this so long as they stay in front of me. So in this manner, we progress for some distance, heading gently uphill.

But then I spy two walkers appearing over the brow of the hill ahead and heading towards me; and the herd spots them at the same time. They stop and look around, clearly troubled by having people both ahead and behind. They start milling and are looking trapped, uncertain what to do, which way to go. I sense they are about to stampede to escape with their calves, and I am downhill behind them, so I am fearful they will be coming straight for me at any moment. Should I run, should I stand still, should I just continue gently walking? This could be about to bring an abrupt end to my trip.

MY JOURNEY SO FAR

This book is the story of my solo wild camping trip walking the 128kms (80 miles) Skye Trail in May 2019 at the age of 69. This was my longest and most challenging solo camping trip to date, though not my introduction to long-distance trekking, hill walking or wild camping. So what led me to attempt this challenge?

My walking experience dates back some sixty years to my time in the Boy Scouts where I learnt so much, though probably did not appreciate it at the time. Since then I have walked and camped extensively in the Lake District, and am currently close to completing all 214 fells in Wainwright's famous series of illustrated guides. Some people are dismissive of 'hill bagging', decrying it as walking for the sake of ticking off fells from a list, rather than walking for the pleasure and experience.

I have some sympathy with this view when people treat it as a competitive exercise, working out how quickly they can complete the full list, and even buying guides which provide the most efficient routes for ticking off as many as possible in the shortest space of time.

But for me, it has added to my pleasure of walking in the Lakes. I plan all my own routes and spend many hours studying Ordnance Survey maps looking at topography and terrain to decide on a route which takes in as many summits as practicable, but also giving me an enjoyable day's walking and gets me back to my starting point.

It has encouraged me to explore less frequented areas of the Lakes I would never otherwise have considered, and I have discovered hidden and deserted gems. Moreover, it motivates me to get up and out when otherwise I might be inclined not to make the effort. But my trips to the Lakes have usually been no more than one or two nights, and staying at recognised campsites, youth hostels or even B&Bs if I am feeling soft.

But over the past decade I have also started taking on greater challenges. In 2009 I walked the West Highland Way with my son, camping or staying at hostels. We omitted the first stage, so walked 105kms (63 miles) over five days carrying all our gear. None of these Sherpa baggage services for us! At the finish we climbed Ben Nevis for good measure.

In 2010/2011 I walked the Coast to Coast path with my daughter (at her instigation), split into two stages over successive years. We carried all our personal gear, but stayed at B&Bs, so no tent or cooking gear to weigh us down. This was 320kms (192 miles) over 14 days.

Also in 2011, I walked the Dalesway with my wife from Ilkley in Yorkshire to Bowness in the Lake District, 133kms (80 miles) over six days. This was in celebration of our 30th wedding anniversary (I know how to treat her), but torrential rain for much of the trip rather spoilt it, especially for her.

My daughter again gets the credit for my progressing to more ambitious overseas treks at higher altitudes. She asked if I fancied climbing Kilimanjaro, and of course the answer was 'Yes'. So in 2015 we climbed Kilimanjaro with an organised tour group. You can read about this in my blog to be found at: www.buster.wordpress.com.

The trek lasted eight days and we climbed from a starting altitude of 2750m to Uhuru peak, the summit of Kilimanjaro at 5895m. The final summit ascent was tough, mainly because of the altitude, but also the temperature at -10° and setting off at midnight with no proper sleep. But the exhilaration, when all 15 of us in our group made it to the summit, was worth it. It whetted my appetite for more high altitude trekking which led, two years later, to my next trip.

This was in 2017 to Nepal for a trek lasting 18 days to Everest Base camp and also crossing three high passes and reaching two summits. It was a demanding and lengthy high altitude trip, and I considered carefully before deciding to take on such a challenge. But I need not have worried, it was demanding, but I made it without any problems despite being the oldest member of the group. You can read about it in my blog: www.nepal623.wordpress.com. Or in more detail in the book I published entitled 'Trekking in Nepal: A personal story and practical guide' which can be purchased in paperback or e-book on Amazon: http://tiny.cc/kvy94y.

These adventures have been the highlights of my outdoor experiences to date, but I had wanted to try more independent trekking, less reliant on porters, guides and using commercial companies to make all the arrangements. I wanted more solitude and natural beauty, less commercialisation and crowds.

I had already dipped my toe into wild camping with a few single night camps in the Lake District, so decided it was time to take on a more substantial walk. In 2018, I completed the East Highland Way, my first multi-night solo wild camping trip. You can read about this in my report on the Walk Highlands website: http://tiny.cc/vyy94y.

I modified the route, which officially starts at Fort William, by omitting the first two stages and instead substituted an alternative start from Rannoch station, in the middle of Rannoch Moor, a National Heritage site and one of the last remaining great wildernesses in Europe. I joined the East Highland Way after two days at the west end of Loch Laggan and followed it east to finish at Aviemore. This made a distance of 113kms (67.8 miles) over six days, though day one included travel from Manchester, so all but 10kms of the total was walked over the subsequent five days, an average of 21kms per day. I carried all my gear and wild camped all the way until my arrival in Aviemore when I treated myself to a night in a hotel.

I enjoyed the trek, but the best part for me was the first two days across Rannoch Moor, not part of the official route. These days were the most remote, beautiful and exciting. Thereafter, much of the walking was low level, through Forestry Commission plantations, along forest roads or on public roads. Finding a wild camping site was not always easy. One night was spent camped in a narrow wooded area between a road and a golf course, and another in a graveyard behind a church! This was not wild camping as I had envisaged it.

So the stage was set for this challenge: the Skye Trail. I knew I wanted to wild camp in more remote and beautiful areas whilst completing a long distance route. The Walk Highlands website was invaluable in helping me choose. It lists 33 long distance trails in Scotland, with detailed maps and information for each one.

I briefly considered the Cape Wrath trail, but rapidly discarded it. It is 370kms long (though one can opt for shorter sections), and has the reputation of being Britain's toughest long distance walk. To quote from the Walk Highlands website:

'The trail is completely unmarked and passes through extremely wild and rugged terrain, far from services and facilities for much of the distance. There are some sections which are pathless and a high degree of navigational skill is required. Walkers need to be self-sufficient and to carry food needed between resupply points. There are also several unbridged river crossings which can become dangerous or even impossible in spate conditions.'

I know my limitations and I judged this to be beyond my capabilities, so I looked at various other possibilities. The West and East Highland Ways were already ticked off, and the Skye Trail was selected as being sufficiently remote and challenging, but not so difficult as to be foolhardy, and with various options to curtail it and take the bus if the weather really turned nasty.

This is the story of my trip, together with practical advice and guidance to help others considering a similar venture. It is not primarily aimed at the expert hill walker or mountaineer (though they are very welcome to read it) as it may be judged too basic by them. However, there are many millions of people who enjoy being outdoors and walking in the hills, but are not necessarily highly experienced or confident. If this is you, I hope it will inspire and inform, and also help keep you safe.

I also hope it will be read and enjoyed by anyone who has no desire or ability to undertake the challenge of the Skye Trail, but who enjoys reading stories of others taking on life's adventures. It is to encourage people to stay young at heart, keep fit and healthy, and not to let age alone put you off living your dreams. Inevitably, as the body gets older no one can stand Canute-like against the sometimes harsh physical realities of ageing, but nevertheless if you are sensible and realistic, then you can tackle far more than you might imagine with self-belief, confidence and planning.

Finally, it is written for myself as a permanent record of my journey and as something to inspire my children and grandchildren.

THE SKYE TRAIL

The Skye Trail is a challenging unofficial long-distance route aimed at experienced hillwalkers, taking in some of the very finest landscapes on the Isle of Skye. It is 128kms (80 miles), starting at the very northern point of Rubha Hunish and taking in the southern coast at Elgol before finishing at the town of Broadford in the south-east corner. The following description is taken from the Walk Highlands website:

'There are no waymarks for the route and many sections do not even have a path. The route includes a long ridge traverse - a very strenuous journey with no easy escape routes - whilst other sections cross burns which become impassable when in spate. The approach to Elgol is on an airy coastal path that requires great care. This walk should be left to the more experienced who can judge the conditions for themselves and are competent with map and compass.'

You have been warned!

I walked it in the conventional direction, north to south, though it can also be completed in the other direction. The advantage of starting in the north is that the toughest, longest and highest section - Trotternish Ridge - is faced on Day 2, when your legs are, hopefully, still fresh. Also, you end in the village of Broadford with accommodation, shops, restaurants and hotels, so you can celebrate the end of your journey. By contrast, there is nothing at Rubha Hunish apart from the old coastguard lookout, now a bothy. If you finish here you will have to make your own way back to civilisation.

The Official Route of The Skye Trail

For those who want to follow the stages as given in the guide book, they are listed with descriptions from the Cicerone guide.

Stage 1. Rubha Hunish to Flodigarry. 11.5kms
The trail starts from Skye's most northerly tip, Rubha Hunish, and follows a spectacular but rough section of the coastline above dramatic cliffs to reach Flodigarry.

Stage 2. Flodigarry to The Storr. 28.5kms
This very arduous and challenging stage climbs from Flodigarry beneath the amazing rock formations of The Quiraing before continuing south on the Trotternish Ridge towards The Storr and a final descent to the road and bus stop. There are no services on this section and no accommodation at the end.

Stage 3. The Storr to Portree. 14kms
This stage takes a short section of road to an unpromising start across rough moorland at the coast. This leads to a fabulous walk along the top of dramatic coastal cliffs with superb views and ends in Portree, the largest town on Skye.

Stage 4. Portree to Sligachan. 19kms
This stage starts along the salt marsh at the edge of Portree bay and then follows the minor road past the small settlements that make up the Braes. From the road end a rough path is followed along Loch Sligachan to the Sligachan Hotel.

Stage 5. Sligachan to Elgol. 18kms
This stage follows remote Glen Sligachan to the beautiful bay at Camasunary. From here you take a cliff path with fantastic views across the water to the Cuillins before you reach Elgol.

Stage 6. Elgol to Torrin. 16.5kms
This stage follows the road for a short section between Kirkibost and Keppoch where a path to a clearance village leads to a final longer road section around the head of Loch Slapin to Torrin.

Stage 7. Torrin to Broadford. 20kms

The final stage follows the coast from Torrin to the cleared villages of Suisnish and Boreraig before heading inland to pick up the Marble Line, the old railroad route into Broadford.

However these stages are not matched in length, ranging from 11kms to 28.5kms. Moreover, the longest is also the hardest, along the Trotternish Ridge. If you are wild camping, there is no need to finish at the suggested stage points, indeed these are not the places best suited to finding an idyllic wild camping spot.

You can read about my alternative planned stages in the next chapter. However, as you will discover in the story of my walk, my plans were soon revised once I started.

PLANNING

For me, the planning at home on the kitchen table, whether preparing for a long trek or just for a few Wainwrights in the Lakes, is part of the pleasure of the outdoors. The anticipation adds to the overall enjoyment.

It also vital for safety if you are trekking alone as I was, in remote areas where the weather can be changeable and unpredictable, even in the summer. So once the Skye Trail was selected I started my planning.

The first stage in planning is to get the right maps. I purchased Harvey's Skye Trail map (£14.50), which covers all of the Trail at a scale of 1:40,000 on one double-sided map, clearly laid out and with the Trail marked so it is easy to follow. It is printed on polyethylene making it tough and waterproof, vital if you are trying to read it on a rainy, windswept ridge; and it comes in a plastic sleeve to keep it dry and safe in your sack. A disadvantage is that it covers the Trail in a linear fashion, so the bigger picture is not visible if you want to get an overall view of Skye.

If you prefer OS maps, you will need Landranger 23 and 32 (£14.99 each in weatherproof version) at a scale of 1:50000 or Explorer 408, 410 and 411 (£8.99 each, but not available in waterproof version) at a scale of 1:25,000. Whichever you decide to take, do not go without a map.

The next vital resource is the Cicerone guide book 'Walking the Skye Trail' by Helen and Paul Webster. This is the same couple who provide the Walk Highlands website (www.walkhighlands.co.uk), an excellent and free interactive guide to hundreds of Scottish walks, including full details for the Skye Trail.

The guide book provides details of the route with their seven suggested stages, and also information on accommodation, villages, places to eat, transport, history and wildlife. For each stage detailed route descriptions are provided to help you avoid getting lost.

My third source of information and advice was the Facebook groups Wild Camping UK and Wild Camping in Scotland. These are closed groups (but you just need to ask to join and agree to the simple rules to be accepted) with 46,000 and 15,000 members respectively. They have a wealth of information, ideas and inspiration. There are review sections for tents, sleeping bags and rucksacks, and you can seek advice on any topic related to Wild Camping and get useful replies.

So my planning was guided by these resources: Harvey's Skye Trail map, the Walk Highlands website, The Cicerone guide and the two Facebook groups. As I always do, I created a spreadsheet on my computer to plan each stage of the trip with distances, stopping points, options for eating and re-supply and possible water sources.

My Planned Stages

I divided the trail into six stages, not the seven suggested in the guide book. However, as I was intending to start in the morning of the first day from Rubha Hunish, I judged this was possible. The Guide Book assumes you will travel to this northernmost point on Day One before beginning the Trail proper. Travelling to Rubha Hunish the night before meant I would get a prompt start and could walk beyond Flodigarry (the first overnight stop in the guide book) and get up and onto the Trotternish ridge for my first night camping on the Trail. (In the event this was not how it worked out, but more of that later.)

Getting beyond Flodigarry on the first day would enable me to break up the lengthy suggested second stage along the Trotternish ridge, and enjoy the experience of true wild camping on 'one of the best ridgewalks in

Great Britain'. I also planned to camp a second night at the southern end of the ridge before descending below The Storr, which would reduce my longest day of walking along the ridge to 18.5kms, compared with the full 28.5kms as the guidebook suggests.

Another consideration in my planning was the wish to spend a night in Portree, the largest town on Skye. This was so I would have a chance to look around, stock up on supplies, enjoy a meal and spend a night in a campsite after a night in a bothy and two wild camping on the ridge.

My plan did require the final four guidebook stages to be compressed into three. However, as the second half is lower, flatter and I reasoned easier than the first half, I judged that an average of 24.5kms (14.7 miles) for each of the last three days was manageable, compared to the relatively leisurely 18.4kms (11 miles) in the guidebook. In summary, my planned stages were:

Stage 1. Rubha Hunish to slightly beyond Uig/Staffin road car park. 18kms
This would take me 6.5kms beyond Flodigarry up to the Quiraing and to the start of the Trotternish Ridge.

Stage 2. Uig/Staffin road to Hartaval (before the Storr on the Trotternish ridge). 18.5kms
Along most of the Trotternish Ridge and camping just before The Storr.

Stage 3. Hartaval to Portree. 18kms
Descending from The Storr and continuing along the coastal path to Portree.

Stage 4. Portree to Loch Dubha (6kms after Sligachan). 25kms
This would be the first of my long days, completing the full Guide Book stage to Sligachan and then another 6kms beyond along Glen Sligachan.

Stage 5. Loch Dubha to Loch Slapin (2kms before Torrin). 26.5kms
My longest day, completing the Guide Book stage to Elgol and then
continuing another 14.5kms almost to Torrin.

Stage 6. Loch Slapin to Broadford. 22kms
The final day would be a short walk into Torrin and then the rest of the
final Guide Book stage to the finish at Broadford.

However, the reality turned out differently. The final three days did
match my plan, but I went beyond Rubha Hunish and on to Flodigarry
for night one, prompted by considerations described in a later chapter.
This allowed me more time on the ridge and a rest afternoon in Portree to
relax, recover and visit the town.

Overnight camping stops

Having planned my six stages, the next task was to locate potential
overnight stops. Night three was fixed as the Torvaig campsite just north
of Portree. There are also campsites at Flodigarry and Sligachan, but
these did not fit into my stages (unless needed in an emergency), and in
any case I wanted to experience wild camping more than campsites.

The Walk Highlands website was helpful here. For each walk, members
can post reports of the route, as I did for my East Highland Way trip:
http://tiny.cc/vyy94y.

These reports make fascinating reading and include a wealth of useful
information and ideas, including places where people camped, or
conversely locations where there was little scope for comfortable wild
camping. I listed all the suggested places for overnight stops from these
trip reports, and cross-referenced with my planned stages to identify
locations which could fit with my plans.

But not all the trip reports give detailed locations. For example, they
might say 'we found a beautiful spot shortly after Sligachan' or 'we
camped on one of the summits half-way along the Trotternish Ridge' or
'there were prettier camping spots further up'.

So the next step was to get out the Harvey map to try and identify more accurately possible locations looking at the contours and terrain; and then to use Google Earth in 3-D view, which is a great resource for translating the image from the map into a picture of the terrain. If one tilts the Google earth view, you can fly over the landscape like a drone viewing the ground below.

Of course, no amount of planning with a map or Google earth can fix a potential camping spot with certainty. It depends on your level of fatigue, the weather and wind conditions as well as on-the-ground observation. But it helps enormously to have surveyed and considered options, so as you walk you can be looking out for potential sites before making a final decision.

Water

You can survive 24 hours without food; you might be a bit hungry, but otherwise you will be fine. Water is a different matter. You would be very thirsty after 24 hours without fluids, especially if you are undertaking strenuous physical activity such as hill walking and carrying all your gear; and even more so in hot weather. So water is always a prime consideration, but it is heavy.

One litre weighs one kilogram. Research suggests people in a temperate climate undertaking normal amounts of physical activity should be drinking between 2.5 to 3.5 litres per day. So on the hill, and in hot weather it will be more. But no one wants to be carrying 4 litres of water unless absolutely necessary. So it is a balance between carrying as little as possible whilst ensuring you don't run out; refilling on route either from natural sources or at pubs, cafes or even private houses on the way.

I take a water filter with me (see the chapter 'On the Trail' for more information) but one needs a water source. Although Scotland has more than its fair share of rain, if it soaks into the ground or disappears in a bog, it is of little use; you need a stream or loch. So it is back to studying the map and Google earth and seeking advice from the Wild Camping Facebook groups.

From this information, I estimated how many potential watering opportunities there were on each stage of my walk. The most difficult stretch was along the Trotternish ridge. Being a ridge, water flows away downhill on both sides, but does not settle along the ridge line. Why would it? And as I was planning on spending two nights on the ridge with no opportunity to refill apart from natural sources, I had to plan carefully.

I was planning on stopping for lunch at Flodigarry before starting the ascent up to the ridge, so knew I could fill my bottles there. After the descent from the ridge at The Storr there was Loch Leathen to replenish supplies. So I had about 48 hours on the ridge when I would need to keep myself hydrated. But I certainly did not want to carry eight litres.

I posted a question about the availability of water on the ridge on both the Wild Camping Facebook sites. The replies varied: 'water is hard to come by', 'a small waterfall about halfway along, but you have to look carefully', 'water isn't too bad, some sources at bealachs', 'we managed to find water but had to go a little off trail', and 'there should be good sources'. Although differing in certainty, they gave me sufficient confidence that I would find some water sources on the ridge, so did not need to carry more than my normal two litres and could refill at some points as I walked. In the event this confidence was misplaced.

After the ridge, water sources looked more readily available as the Trail descends to lower levels and water is flowing down into lochs and streams.

Food

After water, food is the next consideration. There are various points on the route where food can be purchased - Flodigarry, Portree, Sligachan and Elgol - so it was not necessary to carry food for a full six days walking. However, you should check opening times of cafes and restaurants, especially in winter, and calculate when you expect to arrive. The Blue Cabin cafe in Torrin, for example, does not open until noon on Sundays (according to its website), the day I had hoped to arrive to enjoy a hearty breakfast, and is closed Tuesdays 'and occasional other days', so always carry a bit of spare food just in case you arrive on an 'occasional other day'!

I calculated that for my six days' walking I needed to carry five breakfasts, five dinners and three lunches; plus snacks for nibbling whilst walking and tea and coffee. Information on my choice of foods can be found in Chapter five 'On the Trail'.

Travel

Obviously your travel arrangements will depend on where in the country or abroad you are starting. But whatever the specifics of your journey, it needs to be part of your planning process. Skye is not the easiest place to get to for most people. It is a long way north and not especially well-served by public transport. Moreover, even when on Skye, if you are doing the Skye Trail you need to get to the start at Rubha Hunish, which is in the far north of the island and not on any roads.

I will describe the thinking that went into my planning, starting from Bolton, north of Manchester. My preference was for public transport, to do my bit for the environment and to avoid driving some 400 miles. But when I examined the options it was not easy.

The train from Manchester to Kyle of Lochalsh (still on the Scottish mainland) takes 11 hours, involves three changes and arrives at 20.30. This would mean an overnight at Kyle of Lochalsh and then much of the following day travelling by bus to Portree and then to Duntulm, the nearest spot to start walking to Rubha Hunish to actually start the Trail proper.

Alternatively, I investigated the option of a train to Glasgow, a journey time of 3h 50m, and then a bus to Skye. However, the first bus I could catch from Glasgow did not depart until 15.00 and arrived in Portree at 21.40, a bus journey of 6h 40m. So it would be 10pm before I got to any accommodation, too late to eat, though I would at least be on Skye.

Then I considered flying to Inverness. A flight from Manchester departs at 8.40am (meaning 6.40am at the airport and a 5.40am departure from home by taxi) and arrives at Inverness at 9.55am. I would then have to travel into Inverness centre from the airport and either catch the train to Kyle of Lochalsh, arriving 16.12 or the bus to Portree arriving 17.15. Obviously the bus to Portree was the better option as it got me onto Skye, but still an overall travel time door to door of almost 12 hours: taxi - plane - transfer bus to City centre - bus to Skye. An expensive and tiring proposition; and another consideration was that gas canisters cannot be taken on planes, so I would need to stock up in Portree (and leave any unused containers behind at the end).

So finally, I decided to drive from home to Broadford, where the walk finishes, stay the night there and leave my vehicle for my return, take a bus to Portree and another bus to Duntulm the next day, walk to Rubha Hunish and stay overnight in the bothy, ready to start the walk the following morning.

I have given my travel planning in some detail, not because I expect my readers to be making the identical journey, but to illustrate the need for careful planning and the study of timetables to get you to the start of the Trail, and of course to get you home again at the end.

Accommodation

You may decide to camp or hostel from start to finish, but I like to reward myself at the end of a trip with a night in a hotel or B&B to clean off, change into fresh clothes and have a good meal and a beer.

Be warned, accommodation on Skye gets booked up months in advance, even out of high season, so forward planning is necessary. Do not just turn up in the hope of finding somewhere.

So I booked myself into Carrick Bed and Breakfast in Broadford (http://www.lochalsh.net/carrick/) for my first and last nights. The owners are a delightful Dutch couple who have run the business since falling in love with Skye on a holiday seventeen years ago. They allowed me to leave my vehicle on their drive for my return, with a bag of fresh clothes.

Kit

You will find endless discussions online asking for kit recommendations. 'What's the best two-person tent?', or 'What are the best walking boots?' or sleeping mat, or stove, or tarpaulin or just about anything else you might be considering taking on a trek. But you will find almost as many different recommendations as there are replies; and then as many disagreements from people with differing views.

It is like asking for recommendations for 'the best car' or 'best camera'. It all depends on what you want to use it for, how much you want to spend and where, when and how you will be using it. So I will not attempt to offer specific advice on a particular tent or sleeping bag, but will just share some of my thoughts based on personal experience and then give you my personal list.

If you are driving to a campsite and staying there, then you can take everything except the kitchen sink; and some people even seem to include this! But if you are wild camping and carrying everything on your back, there is a fine balance between taking what you want, or might need, whilst taking as little as possible to keep the weight down.

Ultra hardcore, wild campers will take little more than a tarpaulin, a bivvy bag and a stove, weighing in at just a few kilos. When Ernest Shackleton abandoned his ship Endurance on his doomed Antarctic expedition, he allowed each man to take just 2lbs of personal possessions; and he granted this allowance only reluctantly, but recognised that morale needed to be maintained amongst his crew as they prepared for a 350 mile trip hauling heavy sledges across ice floes at temperatures down to -30°F. Shackleton was still in Fahrenheit, but that is -35°C.

But for wild campers who still want a modicum of warmth, comfort and protection against the elements, then the challenge is to keep the weight as low as possible whilst remaining practical, sensible and not breaking the budget.

A useful website is www.ultralightoutdoorgear.co.uk, which is an online outlet specialising in lightweight camping and walking gear. They have a wide range of products, and within each category - sleeping bags for example - you can list items in ascending weight order. However, do not be surprised if the lightest - featuring high-tech materials - is also the most expensive. So for example, a sleeping bag weighing 480g might be over £400 whilst one with the same comfort rating but weighing 1210g could be yours for £120.

This same dilemma, of cost versus weight, applies across the board. Do you want a 2-person tent weighing just 526g for £620 or one weighing 2500g for £200? But weight and cost are not the only parameters for a crucial item such as a tent; you must also consider if it is 'fit for purpose'. An all-season free standing dome tent comes in at a whopping 3000g and £1000, but might be exactly what you need for serious wild camping in extreme conditions.

So for every item of gear you must decide how much you can afford, how much weight you want to carry and what use it will be. Beware of getting over obsessive about weight saving. A titanium spork (combined knife, fork and spoon) weighs 7g and can be yours for £10. I prefer a plastic picnic spoon weighing virtually nothing and which cost me nothing.

Saving a few grams will make no noticeable difference to your pack weight. However, save 100g or more on a few items and you will soon have shaved a kilogram off your total weight: that's the weight of a bag of sugar (not that I am suggesting you will be taking a bag of sugar, but it's a useful reference point) or a litre of water, that you are not having to carry. I look at everything I am taking and decide if I really need it, and can I reduce its weight? So suncream and biodegradable liquid soap get decanted from their full size bottles into small plastic travel bottles; and I take a miniature size tube of toothpaste. Food is carefully weighed and calculated to be just sufficient for the trek, with a small margin for emergencies. My travel toilet bag is replaced by a plastic freezer bag. Steel tent pegs are replaced with aluminium; and so on.

As well as weight considerations, there is also the dilemma of how much 'what if' kit to take in case of emergencies. You should certainly take a first aid kit, but how comprehensive? A few plasters or a full outdoor kit which can cope with any reasonable emergency on the hills? The same goes for spare clothing. Certainly you need some, but how many extra layers in case you get stuck on the hills in bad weather? And how much spare food? I am not offering prescriptive advice, as it depends so much on your experience and confidence, and when and where you will be walking. But do not scrimp on essential emergency kit just to save weight. You will hopefully bring it back unused and may think I need not have bothered with that. But you never know when you might need it, and that is not the time to regret having left it at home.

The basic items you will need are a rucksack, tent, sleeping bag, sleeping mat, pillow, waterproofs, food, cooking and eating utensils, washing gear, first aid kit, water bottles, torch, map, phone, compass and clothing - base layer, fleece, outer layer, socks, hat, gloves. The Ultralight Outdoor gear website gives a comprehensive list and manages to get it all weighing in at just under 7kgs. Including food, water and fuel they suggest will bring the total weight up to around 10kgs or 22lbs. I find this an impossible target to achieve. I am weighing in at 50% more than this at around 15kgs with food and water. But I don't have ultralight gear. For example, my tent weighs 1700g compared with 856g for the tent given on their suggested kit list. So you must decide for yourself how much you really want to pare down to the bare minimum and at what expense.

How much spare clothing to take depends how fastidious you are; and how tolerant your tent mate is if not camping solo! I am not talking about spare warm clothing in case of a turn for the worse in the weather; but changes of clean clothing. In our modern world we are used to changing our underwear every day, but on a wild camping trek where every gram counts this is not realistic. If you are in warm climes you can rinse a technical t-shirt through in a stream and dry it on the outside of your pack. But perhaps not in Scotland?

Certainly you should take a spare pair of socks to allow rotation and in case you get wet feet. But underwear is more of a personal choice with some people just wearing the same base layer clothing for their entire trip, and accepting by the end they will not smell very pleasant. My preference is to take one spare base layer and a spare pair of underpants. This allows daily rotation to give them a chance to air off, and a dry set in case you get soaked through. It keeps my morale up to have a daily change of clothes, albeit by the end of the week they are coming round for the third or fourth time. The other thought is if you are stopping at a pub or cafe for refreshments, do you want to have a fresher set of clothes in consideration of other customers?

As well as the basics listed above, you may also want to take some 'luxuries'. These might include headphones for music, a Kindle (or a book), Satmap, sunglasses, sandals to let your feet breathe, a small tripod seat or a sit-mat, a notebook and a camera. None of these are essential, but they can add to your enjoyment, and in the end that is what most people seek when walking in the outdoors.

For those who want more detail, here is my kit list. I discuss some of my choices in greater detail in the next chapter 'On the Trail'. I don't pretend it is the ultimate kit list, or especially technical; but it is what I took. This book is for keen 'amateurs' seeking advice and useful suggestions, not highly experienced walkers who should already have their own favourite kit list.

Rucksack - Lowe Alpine Khumbu 65:80
Front pack - OMM Chest Pod
Tent - Vango Blade 100
Walking poles - Leki Sherpa
Sleeping - Quechua S5 sleeping bag rated to 0°C
Gilert pillow, Thermarest Prolite self-inflating sleeping mat
Waterproofs - Mountain Equipment jacket and overtrousers, lightweight gaiters

Cooking - Vango compact gas stove with Optimus clip-on windshield, MSR piezo gas igniter, MSR titanium Titan kettle, insulated mug, plastic spoon

Hydration - Sawyer mini water filter, two 750ml aluminium water bottles, one 500ml plastic bottle

Clothing - Thermal top and long johns, two technical t-shirts, fleece jumper, Keela Scuffers trousers, shorts, Montane gilet, Keela jacket, two pairs of socks, two pairs of underpants, buff, waterproof gloves, baseball cap, Salomon Quest boots

Hygiene - toothbrush and toothpaste, wetwipes, lightweight towel, toilet paper, doggy 'poo' bags, antibacterial hand gel, suncream, Smidge insect repellent, tick removal tweezers, First Aid kit, Compeed blister plasters

Miscellaneous - Harvey's Skye Trail map, compass, Satmap Active 10 GPS, Sony Xperia phone with View Ranger app, single charge power bank, survival 'bivvy' bag, reading glasses, sunglasses, notebook and pen, lightweight torch, Sony Cybershot camera, three AA spare batteries, 'uquip' Trinity folding tripod stool, Kindle.

BOLTON TO BROADFORD

The alarm sounds at 6.30am. The sun is already shining through the curtains, a promising sign. I have been following the forecast daily for two weeks and cannot believe my luck. Sunshine and no rain have been showing, unchanged for the week of my walk. I kept expecting it to disappear as the date approached, but no, it persisted and even more surprising turned out to be true.

I have been getting my kit out in the spare bedroom for a few weeks and had packed almost everything the night before, leaving a list of the few items I needed to load in the morning. I take a cup of tea to my wife, still in bed, and say goodbye.

It is a Sunday, chosen deliberately to avoid traffic. Driving north on the M61 and then M6 is a delight as the sun is shining and the traffic (normally a nightmare on the M6) is so light. I am in good spirits and reach Gretna on the Scottish border in 1h40m. I am always surprised how relatively close the Scottish border is to where I live, and then equally surprised how big Scotland is and how long it takes to get to the Highlands. I still have 270 miles to drive on roads which are progressively slower after Glasgow.

I make my first stop after a couple of hours at an unusually attractive service station with a picturesque lake, and have coffee and a pain au raisin before continuing my journey, now on the A74(M), towards Glasgow. I am so pleased I have chosen a Sunday, as the motorway system around Glasgow always seems like a nightmare to me (though in reality probably no worse than around Manchester or London).

After Glasgow it feels like I am getting properly into Scotland, as I skirt Loch Lomond and place names familiar from my West Highland Way start to appear. The scenery is stunning and the bluebells, bright in the sunshine, continue along the roadside verges for miles. But the roads are now single carriageway, bendy and in places narrow. For a while I am stuck behind a coach with no prospect of overtaking, but when it turns off I find myself on the open road with no one ahead or behind. It makes driving so much more enjoyable and relaxing.

After 4½ hours I take my second stop in a lay-bay to have the lunch and coffee I have brought with me. It is a popular road for motor bikes with a steady stream of them passing by. A chap from the only other vehicle in the lay-by is walking his two small dogs and stops to chat as he passes by me. He asks 'Are you a psychiatrist?', which is almost right as I am a retired psychologist! But he is not as psychic as you might think, as he had spotted my personalised number plate. He had been a psychiatric nurse for many years and was keen to chat.

Continuing my journey, the place names are a roll-call of my West Highland Way trip: Tarbet, Crianlarich, Tyndrum (with the Green Welly stop crowded with motorbikes), Bridge of Orchy and Kings House Hotel. The path is visible in places from the road and walkers are spotted at frequent intervals enjoying the lovely sunshine. Then across the expanse of Rannoch Moor before arriving at the magnificent Glencoe and thence to Fort William. I had decided to fill up with fuel in Fort William as I assumed it would be prohibitively expensive on Skye; but I was wrong. The co-op in Broadford turned out to be a penny a litre cheaper much to my chagrin!

About 10 miles past Fort William I pull off the road to visit the Commando Memorial in Spean Bridge. This is an impressive statue dedicated to the men of the original British Commando Forces of World War II. It overlooks the training areas of the Commando Training Depot established in 1942 at Achnacarry Castle.

If I had walked the first section of the East Highland Way in 2018, I would have seen it then, but as I had chosen to omit this stage and start instead at Rannoch Moor, I want to take the opportunity to visit the memorial on this trip. In the bright sunshine it looks truly magnificent, with the Scottish hills in the background.

The final leg of the journey is a scenic if slow drive along the A87 to the Kyle of Lochalsh and the Skye Bridge. The bridge was opened in 1995, but as a toll bridge, which proved highly controversial. It does seem anomalous that hugely expensive motorway systems are built at public expense, but cross a small stretch of water and a toll is deemed necessary. Eventually, in 2004, following a lengthy campaign of civil disobedience and non-payment, the toll was abolished.

But beware of unintended consequences. Since the abolition of the toll, tourism, the lifeblood of Skye, has increased greatly. This is a mixed blessing. The roads are crowded, there is insufficient parking or accommodation, and the 'honey trap' tourist spots are overcrowded, leading to damage to the natural environment. I was told the influx of camper vans is particularly unpopular. They arrive with all their food and drink on board, bought at home at a large supermarket, park their vans in lay-bys or by the roadside to avoid campsite charges, and empty their waste water wherever they choose. Residents on the island refer to 'before and after the toll', with a certain nostalgic longing for the days when the island was less crowded.

The Commando Memorial in Spean Bridge

Finally, after nine hours (I drove steadily and had four stops) I arrive at Broadford and my accommodation for tonight at Carrick B&B. It is a delightful white painted house up a quiet road about half a mile from the centre of Broadford, and I am warmly greeted by Riet, the wife of Piet, the Dutch couple who have owned it for 17 years since falling in love with Skye on a holiday themselves.

It is spotlessly clean and attractively furnished, with a conservatory, lovely garden and free WiFi. As I unload my overnight bag from my vehicle, Piet comes to say hello, and on hearing of my plans for the next day offers to take my rucksack to the bus station and meet me there, so I can wander round Broadford unencumbered in the morning.

I sort out my gear for the next day and then head into Broadford to eat. The nearby Creelers seafood restaurant is closed on a Sunday (and I will be returning in 8 days' time also on a Sunday) so I head into the centre of Broadford and choose the Harbour Restaurant, a family-run Spanish restaurant, highly recommended on Trip Advisor. Luckily I was reasonably early, as it soon filled up and people were turned away. This was in late May on a Sunday night. I have the fresh Hake washed down with a glass of white wine and the home-made almond tart, before heading back to my bed for the night. Tomorrow I depart and will not be sleeping in a bed again until I return.

BROADFORD TO RUBHA HUNISH
TO FLODIGARRY

My plan for today was to look round Broadford, catch the bus to Portree in time for lunch, then catch a bus in the afternoon to Duntulm and from there make my way to the start of the Trail at Rubha Hunish and spend the night in the bothy, ready for a prompt departure tomorrow morning. In the event things do not work out like this. But first to breakfast at The Carrick.

I make my way down to the dining room off the kitchen to be greeted warmly by Piet acting as 'mine host', with Riet busy in the kitchen, but joining in the conversation from stage left. A big pot of tea is most welcome. At home I start every day with two pints of tea. I had made my breakfast choices the night before. As well as the usual choice of eggs and bacon, I had also selected Stornoway black pudding and haggis; both delicious. I am fuelling up before a week of dehydrated rations. After breakfast, I pay (cash only) for last night and also my return night in a week's time. I joke that if I do not make it back I want a refund! On a more serious note, I leave my route plan with instructions to call the emergency services if I have not returned by 7pm the following Sunday; and my wife's phone number to contact her in this event.

My bus to Portree is not until 11.15am, and as Piet has kindly offered to bring my rucksack to meet me at the bus station at 10.45am, this allows me time to amble into Broadford after breakfast for a look around. There is not a lot to see, and the new Co-op building is an eyesore. It is a metal warehouse without a scintilla of sympathy for the local architecture. How did it get planning permission? I do not need any supplies, having come fully stocked at least till I get to Portree, so do not need to go in. Piet told me it becomes exceedingly busy in summer, especially late afternoon as everyone returns from a day out and wants to stock up on food and drink. But there are not enough people who want to work there, so the queues are terrible. Another example of tourist numbers exceeding the capacity of the island to cope.

I sit in the sunshine on the seashore and write up my diary, before heading along to the bus station which I had been told was in front of the post office. But it is hard to spot, being at the far end of the village and concealed within a store. Once located, I am pleased to find it has a cash machine (no fee) so I can get some extra cash, as I am sensing credit cards and contactless payments have not fully reached Skye yet.

Spot on time, Piet arrives with my sack and wishes me good luck. He has plenty of visitors completing the Trail so knows it well. For some group tours, he drops walkers off at the beginning of the day and picks them at the end, at stage points along the Trail.

I am sitting in the small bus shelter with my rucksack by my side when a car pulls up and asks if I want a lift to Portree. I discover he is the manager of the hostel in Portree, so sympathetic to the needs of backpackers, and with excellent knowledge of the Trail and many other routes in Scotland. He tells me he used to be a keen walker until he got married and had children, since when his opportunities for walking are more restricted. He has completed the TGO Challenge, which involves hiking across Scotland from West to East over two weeks, carrying your food and gear and wild camping. It started in 1980 and has become an extremely popular and legendary event. I am in awe.

He gives me two pieces of advice for my trip. The section of the Trail from Portree to Sligachan is extremely boring, and he advises me to miss it out and do something else. (I had received the same advice from a member of the Wild Camping Scotland Facebook group, so I begin to wonder if I should heed it.) He also said the bothy at Rubha Hunish is very popular, so get there early to grab a place. This concerns me. I have an image of my staying overnight in this isolated bothy on the northernmost tip of Skye overlooking a dramatic headland, in isolation and peace. If it is going to be busy and crowded its attractions diminish. For me, much of the draw of walking and wild camping is the solitude, peace and absence of people.

So by the time I am dropped off in Portree and have the bus station pointed out to me, a Plan B is already formulating in my head. Instead of spending time in Portree and having lunch (I am not hungry anyway after my big breakfast) I could catch an earlier bus, arrive at Rubha Hunish by early afternoon and start my walk immediately.

Some might say my months of careful planning were wasted effort if I can make a change so spontaneously and so early in the trip, but I would beg to differ. It is only because I had spent time studying the route and distances and possible overnight stops that I was able, with confidence and in my head, to decide I would be able to make it to Flodigarry tonight and know I can camp there. So that is what I provisionally decide to do.

The bus to Duntulm departs from Portree at 12.15pm, and the driver is so friendly and helpful. I have an image of bus drivers being surly and grumpy and demanding the exact change. But not this one. A friendly greeting as I board, and he knows exactly where I need to get off: 'At the telephone box. I'll tell you when we get there.' He seems to know many of the locals who board and alight, and I'm sure he stopped wherever they wanted, not always at regular stops. As we pass a bin lorry going in the opposite direction, he stops and has a quick chat to the driver before proceeding. It creates a warm glow to the start of my trip. Thank you to the bus driver.

We are heading north along the east coast of Skye and I get my first view of the Trotternish Ridge. It is visible on our left hand side for the whole of the journey, and it is quite intimidating to think I will be walking back along the top of it over the next three days. It is dramatic and impressive. At the base of The Storr I am shocked at the number of parked cars and camper vans. It is heaving with tourists, all keen to drive as close as they can and then take the path up towards The Storr, though not its summit I am sure. Yet the bus is not even half full. People should make more use of public transport.

The driver calls out 'Shulista Road for the Skye Trail'. This is my stop! I alight, and as the bus departs it fully hits me that this is the start of the trip I have been planning for months. I'm off; and the weather could not be better. The walk to the bothy at Rubha Hunish is only about 2kms, so I take it steady as I get used to walking with my pack, now loaded with an extra 2kgs of water.

The remains of the settlement of Erisco can be seen close to the shore. Crofters moved here following the defeat of the Jacobites at Culloden. The land at Erisco was less fertile than the crofts from which the families had moved, and the village was abandoned in 1765. The ruined building walls are all that remain.

I take in the landscape around me. It is more harsh, stark and severe than the Lakes where I walk most frequently. It is a sunny day today, but it gives the impression it could be brutal in bad weather. Pretty whitewashed cottages are scattered across the countryside, but built to withstand the weather with small windows and thick walls. There are no trees.

The landscape and cottages close to Rubha Hunish

Soon the small bothy at the northern tip of Skye overlooking Rubha Hunish headland comes into view. It is a former coastguard lookout station, standing close to the steep cliff face and with commanding views over the Minch and to the Isle of Lewis and Harris. It was built in 1928, but has been a bothy since the mid-70s. Following storm damage in 2005 it was renovated over a series of years, most recently with the addition of external wooden cladding to part of the building.

Inside it is clean and well-maintained, with a bunkroom for just three people, and a lookout room with windows on three sides giving a panoramic view of the sea. I put my rucksack on the top bunk to stake a claim, but note another sleeping bag and a pair of shoes already inside on the floor, so at least one other occupant. I am mindful of the advice that it becomes crowded, and I have pretty much decided to press on to Flodigarry tonight.

But first I want to explore the headland, described in the guide book as 'one of the most magical spots on Skye', not just press on in haste. I leave my rucksack in the bothy and descend towards the cliff edge and the steep path which leads down onto the headland. However, I decide against continuing all the way to the headland itself. It is a steep descent and then ascent to return, and I estimate will take a couple of hours to explore properly. Instead I take in the view and return to the bothy having finally decided I will indeed continue further today rather than stopping overnight.

The lookout bothy at Rubha Hunish

Back in the bothy I have a drink and a snack, and two other walkers arrive, confirming that this would be a crowded place to sleep, not the quiet solitude I had imagined. So I retrieve my rucksack and head south, the official start of the Skye Trail. It is 3pm. I am heading to Flodigarry, 11.5kms away and with an estimated walking time of 5½ to 6½ hours according to the Guide Book, so I need to get moving.

A gusty wind is blowing with sufficient strength to buffet me sideways as I walk. I would not want to be camping up here, even though it is a fine sunny day. Two walkers heading in the opposite direction are going to the bothy for the night, it will be getting more crowded.

The route follows the cliff-top coastal path with dramatic views to the rocky coastline below. It passes the ruins of St Moluag's church and heads across to an isolated whitewashed cottage close to the shore before rising up again to a Second World War radar station. The wind drops by late afternoon and the shadows slowly lengthen as I descend a steep rake returning to the foreshore and head towards Staffin Bay and the tiny settlement of Flodigarry.

The dramatic north coast

I arrive at the hostel at 7pm, four hours after setting off from the lookout bothy, earlier than I had expected. The hostel is a sparkling white building looking out to sea with views of Flodigarry Island and the Torridon hills beyond. People are sitting on the terrace basking in the evening sun, having a drink and reading. It is a tranquil atmosphere, but I want to get set up and have something to eat.

Inside is a notice saying 'Back in 30 minutes', which is not very helpful unless the start time is also given! So I make myself a cup of tea in the hostel kitchen and wander back out to the terrace. I cannot see any tents, otherwise I would just pitch up. A German walker arrives, also planning on camping, so the two of us wait for the manager to return from his dinner 'in 30 minutes'.

When he does, it transpires the small neatly mown field at the back of the hostel is for tents, but with no one else there it was not recognisable as a campsite. I pitch my tent opposite the German walker and head inside to rehydrate my pulled pork and rice dinner, followed by chocolate pudding with chocolate sauce, then return to my tent. At least my first night is being spent in some comfort, albeit not in a bothy as planned.

ON THE TRAIL

Once all your planning is complete, and the tortuous decisions on what kit to take and what can be left behind have been made and everything is packed, you are finally off and walking. A sense of relief and enjoyment floods over you, unless it is cold, wet and windy in which case you might be thinking 'Why am I doing this?' As you walk, there are practical matters to consider. Safety and Navigation are sufficiently important to justify a chapter each in their own right, so this chapter covers a miscellany of other topics.

Walking poles

These are a topic of discussion and disagreement. I used to be rather snooty about them. This was based on seeing organised groups of 'ramblers' in the Lake District walking along a flat, paved path by the shore of a Lake, all walking with their poles - click, click, click. It seemed more of an affectation than an aid to walking. But I was converted (though still not for flat walking on tarmac) when I trekked up Kilimanjaro, and have since used them in Nepal and regularly when walking in the Lakes. On ascents and descents they add stability, take strain off the knees and give extra support and leverage.

But some people hold opposing views and believe they are just something extra to carry, an encumbrance, and can lead you to rely too much on the poles, risking a fall if the poles slip. There is also a view that they leave holes in soft ground and scratch rocks, damaging the environment. So you must decide. But I would advise you to at least try them out, both ascending and descending, because if you have not yet used them you may find them a revelation.

However, on flattish ground they are not necessary, and on very steep ground, where you need to scramble or use your hands for extra grip and stability, they become a liability. One sees people with sticks flailing as they use their hands for support whilst scrambling up rocks. So you need to be able to stow and retrieve your poles as the terrain varies. Osprey sacks have a system which allows poles to be stowed easily without removing the pack. This is a great boon. Most other packs have loops on the rear of the pack, necessitating its removal to store or retrieve your poles.

Front pack

For many years I had struggled with where to carry all those small essential items you need ready access to during a walk. Things like map, compass, GPS, phone, camera, glasses, sunglasses, suncream, energy bar etc. If you keep them in your rucksack, you are forever having to take it on and off. If you stuff them in your pockets they bulge, are uncomfortable and in danger of getting lost; and if wearing shorts and a t-shirt in hot weather there are simply not enough pockets.

I considered a waist belt, but these are not practical with a rucksack, as the waist strap on the sack is exactly where the waist belt would be. There are chest harnesses used by fell runners which can carry a couple of water bottles as well as enough room for map and emergency clothing. But these are worn over your shoulders, exactly where the shoulder straps from your sack need to sit.

Finally, I have found a solution. The Chest Pod from Original Mountain Marathon. It weighs only 95gms and has a 4 litre zip pocket and a quick access map pocket. It attaches to the front of your rucksack with four short cords, so does not interfere with any of the straps on your sack. It is designed for OMM packs, but most rucksacks have a variety of loops on the straps so it is not a problem to attach. I use two mini carabiners on my shoulder straps for the upper attachments, and clip the lower ones onto the base of the shoulder straps. It has improved my walking experience immensely. I can now access all my useful items instantly without the need to stop, and as a result take more pictures, check my position more frequently and put suncream on when needed.

Are you sitting comfortably?

Eating, reading or just sitting on flat ground without any backrest or support is uncomfortable. So although it is not essential and adds weight, I take a lightweight tripod folding stool. It weighs 260g, but is worth it to be able to eat a meal in a degree of comfort. It doesn't have a backrest so I can't lean back, but it gets my body above my feet so I can sit in balance with my food on my knees. Of course, a convenient rock serves the same purpose, but there never is one just when you want it.

A lighter weight alternative is a sit-mat, but this does no more than insulate your bottom and provide slight padding; it does not allow sitting comfortably unless you place it on a rock. Another option is to buy a conversion kit which bends your sleeping mat into the shape of a chair, but as with a mat, your feet are not below your body so it does not allow you to sit upright comfortably; nor can you lean back with confidence. If you want the luxury of a proper folding chair with legs and a backrest, then you are up to about 500g in weight. But I recommend taking something to be able to sit on to eat, read, write or just enjoy the sunset.

Keeping clean

What do you take in your wash kit? Do you even take a wash kit? Keeping clean whilst wild camping is important for health, but more so for comfort and morale. I couldn't go a week without brushing my teeth, so a toothbrush and paste have to be included.

Soap, if you take it should be biodegradable (though some people doubt the wisdom of even biodegradable soap), but my preference is for wet-wipes. (Which are disposed of only once I get back to civilisation - 'Leave No Trace'.) They are quite heavy being moist, but the luxury and comfort of having a freshen-up in the tent each morning and night is worth it. Just recall how lovely it is when you get a fresh wipe from the steward on a long-haul flight. It also saves taking soap and needing to find a water source to have a wash.

I also take a small plastic bottle of hand sanitiser gel; and toilet paper in a plastic bag to keep it dry. I have a beard so do not need a razor. Can you go a week without a shave? For some people a razor gives the same fresh feel as wet wipes do for me, and is considered indispensable.

If you are planning on stopping at a pub or cafe, make sure you avail yourself of the facilities; or public toilets if the opportunity exists. But there will be times when nature calls and you are on the hills. For a 'pee' just make sure you are well away from any water source, footpath or area where people might stop to rest. For a 'poo' the advice is normally to take a trowel and dig a hole. This should again be well away from any water source, path or frequented area.

But in my experience a lightweight trowel is often insufficient to make any impact on the firm ground. A more robust shovel would be too heavy. So my preference is to find a natural hole, hollow or dip, well away from any water source or anywhere people might sit, walk or camp, and then fully cover the waste with soil, rocks or vegetation. But, most importantly, used toilet paper is placed in a black plastic 'doggie bag', which is knotted and taken with me until I find a suitable litter bin.

At night, a 'pee' bottle is a great life improver. You do not want to be getting out of your warm sleeping bag and going outside on a cold or wet night to have a 'pee'. For men at least, the solution is to take a plastic bottle of sufficient capacity to use at night in the tent and then empty outside in the morning. A real life improver.

Food

'An army marches on its stomach' is variously attributed to Napoleon or Frederick the Great. It is important to keep well fed on the hills, to maintain your energy levels and stamina, and also for morale and motivation. Meal stops become an important part of a long day, and you

want to enjoy your food not just eat to stay alive. But weight is as always a consideration when everything has to be carried on your back. Also, fresh food will not keep for long in a warm backpack on a hot summer's day.

The obvious choice is to take dehydrated camping food which is lightweight, nutritious and high in energy. You can dehydrate your own food at home, and there is advice for doing this on the internet. It is cheaper than buying commercially freeze-dried food, but unless you are a regular wild camper the effort is probably not worth it and the cost saving not great.

For an excellent review of some commercial dried foods, have a look at this site: http://tiny.cc/j3y94y. It is found on the website of Tim Moss who is an explorer and adventurer (https://thenextchallenge.org/) which is well worth a visit for inspiration and advice on many topics, not just food. He has undertaken adventures across all continents and shares his experiences freely on his site.

Based on his review of various dried foods, I chose Real Turmat purchased from Base Camp Foods. They are expensive at about £10 per meal, but very tasty, and when solo wild camping an enjoyable meal at the end of a long day is worth the extra cost. They are freeze dried, weigh about 120gms (before adding water), are easy to prepare and can be eaten from the pack, thus eliminating the need to take a bowl. You can buy cheaper meals and ones with more calories per serving, but in the words of Tim Moss on his website 'If I could only choose one ration pack manufacturer then it would be Real Turmat.' Say no more.

For lunches, I took some Real Turmat soups. I have tried pot noodle type meals in the past, which are cheap and lightweight and can be bought in any supermarket, but they are bulky, can easily be crushed, have a long list of additives and don't appeal to my taste buds.

For breakfasts, I struggled to find a satisfactory product. Previously, I have taken my own home-made granola, which is tasty and nutritious. But carrying enough for a week is quite an extra weight when every

100gms counts, and it requires milk and a bowl. I have previously taken powdered milk to mix on the trail, but that requires the powder and a container to mix it in.

Instant porridge, mixed in its pot with boiling water is an obvious choice. Lightweight, inexpensive and high in slow release energy. But I find them unpalatable; not a patch on real porridge. I was not sure I could face eating a tub every morning to set me on my way. So in the end I opted for cereal bars, nutritious and palatable if not very exciting.

For energy whilst walking, I take a selection of nuts, raisins, crisps, energy bars and chocolate. To save weight I only took sufficient for the first three days, knowing I would be visiting Portree on the third night so could replenish my stocks there.

Water

My planning had identified water supply as a potential problem along the Trotternish Ridge, though I gained some (misplaced) reassurance from advice received from the Wild Camping Facebook groups. I normally carry two 750mls bottles and hope to refill them at some point during the day giving me 3ltrs per day for cooking and drinking. However, my uncertainty about being able to refill along the ridge persuaded me to take an extra 500mls bottle. Water is very heavy (1kg per litre), so you do not want to carry more than necessary; but nor do you want to run out.

Some people drink untreated water from fast-flowing streams, just checking for no dead animals upstream; and seem to suffer no ill effects. Mountaineering Scotland advises: 'In general, when in the mountains of Scotland above human habitation, the water is safe to drink, but you do have to think about where it is coming from and follow basic common sense rules.' By contrast, Scottish Water states: 'Water from lochs and rivers may look clean but it needs to be treated before it is safe to drink.' You don't want a stomach upset in a small tent in the hills, so my advice is to treat water before drinking.

There are three main options. Boiling for at least one minute will kill off bacteria but not remove particulates, it uses gas and if you want to drink the water, you need to wait for it to cool down.

A Steripen uses UV light to kill bacteria. It is a hand-held, battery powered device costing around £50, which purifies water in about one minute. It is quick and convenient, but as with boiling it will not remove particulate matter, though will destroy bacteria, viruses and protozoa.

The third option is filtering. There are various brands available, but I opted for the popular Sawyer mini filter, costing around £24. You fill the squeezable container with water from a stream, attach the filter to its neck and then gently squeeze into your drinking bottle. It is small, lightweight and removes all bacteria and protozoa as well as particulates. The main disadvantage is it is fairly slow and tedious having to filter the water from the squeezable bottle into your drinking bottle.

My solution was to keep one of my water bottles for filtered water for drinking on the trail, and the other with untreated water to be boiled before use for making hot drinks or adding to dehydrated meals. I did not take a Steripen.

Midges

Midges (otherwise known as *Culicoides impunctatus* if you must know) are the bane of a summer trip to the Highlands. The males usually arrive late May, but they don't bite. It is the females who will suck your blood! They arrive a week or so after the males, so about early June, and last till about September. But the dates vary depending on weather conditions and climatic variables. You can get a forecast of the risk of midge attack on a five point scale at: https://www.smidgeup.com/midge-forecast/.

The site contains lots of other useful information about the little blighters, and sells its midge repellent Smidge. It claims to have been scientifically tested and proven to be effective against midges (and mosquitoes) for up to eight hours. I have certainly found it effective, but I have never tested it in peak midge season - I just don't go then. But it seems to work for me. Others will tell you nothing works against the 'wee beasties'.

The two main alternatives that regularly get mentioned are DEET based repellents and Avon Skin So Soft. Many people are wary of DEET because it has been reported to have side-effects including rashes, skin irritation, numb or burning lips, nausea, headaches, dizziness and difficulty concentrating. But other reviews have found no evidence of harmful side-effects if used properly, so you must decide. Certainly many people are wary of it and prefer alternatives. (Smidge contains no DEET.)

Although 'Avon Skin So Soft' is not marketed as an insect repellent, and Avon makes no claims for it as such, it has been touted as effective for this purpose for decades. It is reported that Royal Marines swear by it and it is claimed to be highly effective because of the ingredient citronella. But as always, others disagree and insist it has no proven benefits.

Finally, you can prevent them from getting to your face by wearing a mosquito net over your head. They look rather foolish, but a small price to pay to avoid being bitten to death.

The best advice is to avoid the midge season. If you cannot, take whatever works for you. Midges don't fly if the wind speed is more than a few miles per hour. They prefer still, calm conditions and are worse at dawn and dusk and in damp and humid locations. Good luck!

Ticks

Ticks are an increasingly common risk. They are an insect related to mites, spiders and scorpions. They are found in any place with moist air, typically woodland, heathland, moorland and pasture. They cannot jump or fly, but wait for a passing human or animal and then catch on with their hooked front legs. They then search for a nice site to take a bite and start gorging on your blood. The bite is usually painless, so the first you know is when you spot an engorged body swollen to many times its normal size with your blood!

Ticks can carry many diseases, but by far the most common in the UK is Lyme disease. This is an infectious disease which appears on average two weeks after the bite. A red bulls-eye rash may appear around the bite site about a week later with early symptoms of a flu-like virus - headache, fever, aching, stiff neck, muscle pain and tingling sensation. The symptoms can vary, and the disease is not always easy to diagnose, so if you suspect you may have been bitten tell your GP.

Prevention is obviously the best course of action. Try and avoid long grass, wear a long-sleeved shirt and tuck trousers into your socks, use insect repellent and check each night on your clothes and skin for any that have come along for the ride.

If you discover you have been bitten and it is nicely bloated with your blood, do not just grab it and pull it off. That way you squirt all the blood back into your body together with any bacteria. You need to slide something between the tick and your skin to ease it off without squeezing. The best solution is to use one of the widely available tick removal tools. Insert it as close to the skin as possible and gently lift off the offending insect without squeezing or twisting. Wash your skin and hands afterwards.

Electronic devices

For some, the opportunity to escape from the tyranny of modern technology is one of the best reasons for wild camping away from phone signals and internet access. For others, the ability to keep in touch with friends and family and post pictures of beautiful camping spots is part of the pleasure of being away. Whatever group you might be in, a mobile phone is nowadays a vital aid to safety, though with the rider that you should not rely on it, as in many places you may not have a signal.

On the Skye Trail there is a signal for most of the route with the exception of around Torrin. There used to be a public phone box in

Torrin but it has been removed as it was not used enough to justify retaining it, so if you need to make emergency contact when around Torrin you are out of luck.

As well as a mobile phone you may be carrying a GPS device, camera, Kindle and possibly other devices. The one thing they all have in common is the need to keep them charged up. Battery life varies between devices and of course on how much you use them. A Kindle will last a week; a mobile phone may be less than 24 hours. Different devices infuriatingly have different charging leads, so you may need a different lead for each device, though all will normally plug into a USB socket, so you only need to carry one of these.

There can be opportunities to recharge if you stop at a pub or cafe, so take advantage of these whenever you can. Though if you only have one USB plug, then you will only be able to charge one device at a time; and a lunch stop of an hour or so will not be sufficient to fully recharge a dead battery.

So what are the options for recharging on the move? The first is a power bank. This is an external power source which will recharge your phone or other device. There is a trade off between weight and capacity. A high capacity one may recharge your phone up to six times but will be heavy. A single charge one weighs less than 100g and costs about £30. There are many to choose from online. Once depleted, the power bank itself will need recharging from a mains outlet.

The second is a solar charger. A lot of people are rightly critical of the performance of solar chargers, especially some sold on the internet. They produce no more than a trickle charge in bright sunlight and would take days to fully recharge a flat battery.

However, not all are like this. On my trip to Nepal I took a three panel Anker PowerPort. Unfolded, the three panels can be hung on the back of a rucksack and up to two devices can be recharged as you walk (making you very popular with your fellow walkers). In bright sunshine I found an iphone recharged fully in about three hours, and even on cloudy days it still charged in half a day. I became adept at walking (as far as practicable) with my back to the sun, and always propped up my rucksack facing the sun whenever I stopped.

At camp, the charger can be draped on your tent facing the sun. So I would recommend it if you are willing to carry it and think there will be sufficient sun. But for Skye I did not take it. I did not want the extra weight and I was not confident of getting sufficient sunshine to justify taking it on the trip.

I used my phone sparingly (no photos, switched off during the day, airplane mode whilst composing any messages, then send and switch off again) and it still had 70% charge left at the end of the week. My Satmap lasted three days on the charge from home, two further days from a power bank recharge and I then fitted disposable batteries. My camera and Kindle lasted the full trip.

Camera

For many walkers, taking beautiful photos of the scenery, sunsets, sunrises, lakes and mountains (as well as people and yourself) is part of the pleasure of being outdoors. The Facebook groups regularly feature stunning pictures, especially from wild campers in remote locations.

I used to own a Panasonic Lumix G7, which is a good camera but it weighs around 700gms with lens, and on the trek in Nepal I found it increasingly irksome having it hanging around my neck, swinging back and forth as I clambered over the rocky terrain. Moreover, I rarely made use of its many advanced features, leaving it on Auto almost all the time. So I traded it in for a Sony Cybershot weighing 300gms and small enough to carry in a pocket. The battery comfortably lasts for a week, and with a 30x optical zoom it provides great pictures.

Of course, most people nowadays don't even own a camera, using their phone to take pictures and videos, and share them instantly with friends on social media. Modern mobile phones have astonishingly good cameras, they slip in your pocket, are lightweight and eliminate the need to take a separate camera on your trip. But if you rely on your phone to take photos, you will quickly run down the battery, and you may need it in case of an emergency. Also, a phone is more vulnerable to damp and damage than a conventional camera. So if you want to shoot freely as you walk in all weather conditions, then a sturdy but lightweight camera is far preferable to a delicate mobile phone.

FLODIGARRY TO BEALACH CHAIPLIN

Another beautiful day dawns, the sun shining brightly and already quite high in the sky even as I emerge from my tent. I have my usual cup of tea and a cereal bar in the hostel kitchen, and then a hot shower. I head outside onto the terrace for a look out to sea and Flodigarry Island, dramatically illuminated by the sun shining through clouds.

Flodigarry Island silhouetted against the morning sun

I pack up my tent and depart shortly before 9am. Today I will be heading up onto the Trotternish Ridge. The path from the hostel leads to the road I travelled along in the bus yesterday. After a kilometre the path heads off to the right and heads steadily uphill. I pass two small lochs as I approach the astonishing rock formations of the Quiraing.

The rocky formations of the Quiraing with the Needle centre left

Heading past the Quiraing with the Needle over my right shoulder

The triple summit of the Prison is passed on the left, and on the right the Needle. I can take it steadily as I have gained time on my original plan by getting to Flodigarry yesterday. The path, which had been quiet with just a few other walkers this morning, becomes ever busier with people who are obviously not serious walkers. There are families with children, couples in sandals and summer clothes and tourists of many nationalities. I am approaching the car park on the Uig to Staffin road, an access point to walk easily towards the Quiraing.

As I arrive at the car park I am astonished at the number of cars and camper vans. It is packed even in May. Goodness knows what it will be like in mid-summer. I do not hang around, but head across the road to return to peace and tranquillity. I spot a small stream just after the road and take the opportunity to refill my water bottles. I am drinking a lot because of the heat and exertion and know I have another couple of days walking and camping on the ridge ahead.

Looking south towards the Trotternish Ridge

The ridge stretches ahead of me as far as my eye can see. It is not a single smooth ridge, but a spectacular range of hills with 13 named summits over a distance of some 30kms. It undulates up and down and meanders in and out, making for tough walking and the need for careful navigation in poor visibility. The curious topography is a result of basaltic lava flows building up to a depth of some 800m and causing the underlying sedimentary rocks on the eastern side to collapse, tilting everything sideways.

Underfoot the ground is baked dry. Areas which would normally be wet and boggy are dry cracked earth. This eliminates the problem of sinking into the mud but portends a lack of water likely to be found on the ridge. It is harder and slower walking than I had anticipated, and I am glad I pushed ahead yesterday, gaining me extra time for the later stages. I stop for a cooked lunch. This is an innovation for me. Usually I usually have no more than a snack at lunchtime, supplemented by energy bars, crisps, nuts and raisins as I walk. But with the long hours of daylight at this time of the year, I can walk till late if necessary, so have decided to have a proper stop in the middle of the day. I settle down, brew up a coffee and have reindeer soup from a dehydrated packet, using some of my precious water. I sit in the sun and relax.

The summit of Beinn Edra

But I need to keep moving, so clear up, pack on and continue along the trail. It is a long uphill stretch to reach the trig point at the summit of Beinn Edra at 611m. It is 5pm and I am feeling tired, but decide to continue for another hour or so towards four smaller summits which lie ahead.

I pass a small tent already pitched, and recognize it as belonging to the German walker I had met last night at Flodigarry hostel. But I have decided to make a bit more progress before setting up for the night. I approach Bealach Chaiplin, about 9kms before The Storr, the area I had mentally set as my target for today and start looking for a suitable place to pitch my tent. As I look around I see two other tents pitched lower down the ridge on the eastern side. I stay on the top of the ridge but seek some shelter from the wind which is blowing quite hard. It is mostly flat with few opportunities for protection, but I find a patch of flat ground next to a small mound and decide this will do. The wind drops through the evening so I need not have worried.

Camping on the ridge at Bealach Chaiplin

After eating another of my dehydrated meals (and using more water) I am relaxing when three people appear from below the ridge and come over for a chat. They are camping in the two tents I spotted nearby, and have pitched lower down to avoid the wind. They are a German woman and a Canadian couple. She is giving them a taste of wild camping, but they cannot complete the whole Skye Trail as the Canadians have to return home in a couple of days. They too are low on water and tell me there is a source further below them, but an estimated 30 minutes down and a long slog back up. They have come up to sit and watch the sun setting in the west, so we say 'Goodnight' and I head into my little tent.

BEALACH CHAIPLIN TO BEN DEARG

I oversleep this morning having slept through my alarm, but I must have needed it as I feel rested; and it later turns out to be good fortune. Overnight I have been mulling over my water situation. After my morning cup of tea I will have 500mls left. So it is not critical, but certainly not sufficient for another night on the ridge. I could descend at The Storr some 9kms hence, where I am confident there will be water lower down, but I am tempted by an alternative route option which stays on the ridge above The Storr and continues all the way to Portree. This option has the advantages of being more remote, shorter and arriving at the campsite at Torvaig from the north. The alternative coastal route arrives from the south and necessitates an uphill trudge of 1.2kms at the end of the day to the campsite, only to be retraced the following morning to return to the Trail. But without extra water the option of staying high and continuing on the ridge for another night will not be possible.

I am cleaning my teeth when the three nearby campers I met last night hove into view carrying their gear. They head over and tell me that the Canadian man had descended to fetch water and they had brought enough to spare 2 litres for me. The friendship and kindness of fellow walkers is amazing. I am now set up for today at least. If I had not overslept I might have been gone by now and missed them! You never know how things will turn out.

I pack up and set off in bright sunshine once again and soon change into shorts and take off a couple of layers. I wish I had brought my sun hat, but fortunately I do have suncream. It is tough walking, not a straightforward ridge walk, but undulating up and down with some steep sections and some scree. Nothing impossible, but with a heavy pack and in the heat it is slow, hard work.

At points the path is only a metre or less from the cliff edge, so in poor visibility or strong winds caution would be needed, but I am so fortunate with the weather. The view out to sea is of a magnificent blue sky streaked with white cloud formations. After a few hours, I stop for a lunch of soup and coffee and a chance to rest. I find by the afternoon I am flagging, but food and rest soon restore my energy.

Enjoying the morning sunshine with the Trotternish Ridge behind

Sky over Skye

I continue towards The Storr. There is a steep descent down a rocky slope before the long ascent to the highest point on the Trail, the summit of Hartaval at 669m. From here it is down to the pass below The Storr (Bealach a Chuirn) and this is the choice point for either dropping down to the coastal route or staying high and continuing on the ridge to Portree. Water is still the limiting factor. The kindness of my fellow walkers has got me comfortably through today, but I am making slower progress than hoped, so it will require another night on the ridge before I reach Portree if I choose to stay high.

I descend to Bealach a Chuirn and hear the most beautiful sound: running water. There is a small but flowing stream, the first fresh water I have seen since yesterday morning. I fill all my bottles and know I can now continue on the higher route and camp a second night on the ridge before continuing to Portree tomorrow. My spirits soar. I skirt round the southern flank of The Storr and detour to the edge of the rocky cliff face to catch sight of the Old Man of Storr and the Needle before returning to the path to continue heading south.

The Old Man of Storr

The terrain is less hilly than earlier in the day, but the walking is hard because the ground is uneven and covered in coarse tussocks of grass. As the afternoon progresses I am beginning to feel tired, but decide to continue until 6pm. However, when I see the ascent to Ben Dearg

(552m) loom ahead of me, I decide I will save it for tomorrow when my legs are fresh, and instead find a spot for the night now. This is not difficult, as there is plenty of flat ground and with no wind there is no need to find a sheltered spot. I am well into my routine by now, so the tent is quickly erected, my things are inside, sleeping mat inflated and cooking gear ready to use. There is a sense of satisfaction in being organised and efficient. Of course the weather makes it so much easier. If it had been blowing hard or pouring with rain I might not have felt so pleased with myself.

My overnight spot just north of Ben Dearg

A party of three men carrying large rucksacks stop for a chat. They do not appear very fit and are looking hot and tired, but need to continue awhile before stopping for the night, as they have a bus to catch in Portree tomorrow morning. Later a couple arrive, just carrying day packs, so not equipped for an overnight stop, looking anxious about getting to Portree this evening, still a good few hours away. They set off earnestly but will have a late arrival. I think they must have underestimated the challenge of the Trotternish Ridge. The first midges arrive this evening, though not fully fledged Skye midges, mere beginners. A spray of Smidge and a citronella night-light candle deter them. The evening is so still the candle stays alight outside the entrance to the tent without a flicker. Tomorrow I will be at a campsite so can look forward to a hot shower.

NAVIGATION

The Skye trail is not waymarked, and in many places there is no clear path. Visibility can be poor, and in some sections you are exposed to steep drops if you wander off the path. So navigation skills are essential. You must carry an OS or Harvey map and a compass; and know how to use them. If you don't know how to, there are useful resources online such as the excellent OS site https://tinyurl.com/j7kmwx9. Or you can attend a course. It is not rocket science, but you do need to be able to read and understand a map, and know how to use a compass and give a grid reference.

Although I always carry a paper map and compass, I am converted to the ease of using a GPS device. I know some purists will never use anything other than a good old-fashioned paper map, and warn of the dangers of losing a signal, batteries running flat or the device failing; and all of these can happen. Hence the need to always have a map as back-up and be able to use it.

But on a day-to-day basis in the real world, a portable GPS device is so much more convenient. Trying to read a map in a howling gale or torrential rain or at night is nigh on impossible. If you have the map in a map case round your neck in a strong wind you are in danger of being strangled as it blows round and round. And why is the bit of the map you always need just on a fold of the map?

The GPS gives you instantly one crucial piece of information a paper map will not; and that is your location. If you don't know where you are, a map is of little use. At night or in poor visibility or simply when you want to know exactly where you are, a GPS gives you the answer. As you set-off walking an arrow points in your direction of travel and you can see almost immediately if you are heading off course. Another advantage is your route can be downloaded in advance from numerous sites, or you can create your own at home, and it is then displayed on the GPS map display.

It is good practice to revert to map and compass occasionally just to keep your navigation skills fresh, but otherwise my preference is to keep my map in my pack as back-up and use a GPS device.

However, there are some occasions when a map is preferable. Using a GPS device is like looking at a map through a keyhole. You only get to see the small area immediately around you. You can of course zoom out, but as the screen stays the same size the scale diminishes and you rapidly lose definition.

So if you want to get a larger scale overview of the terrain, your journey and your progress, a map is necessary; and for planning your trip at home on the kitchen table a map is essential. Only by opening it out and surveying the whole area can you plan your trip, locating possible camping spots, escape routes, shelter and water sources.

I use two devices, so I have a back-up if one should fail, before needing to get the map out. I have owned a Satmap for many years and it has been worth its weight in gold, ensuring I am on the correct path, or helping me return to my route if I have strayed. It is not cheap at between £400 to £500 depending which model you buy, and you must then purchase SD map cards for your area. These vary in price, but for Skye it was £32, though for larger areas such as the whole of GB the price rises to £154. It is robust and built for outdoor use even if wearing gloves. It can run on rechargeable batteries or disposables. A full charge lasts about three days if you do not use it excessively, after which you need to switch to disposable batteries.

I also have the View Ranger app on my phone. This is a free app, but again you must purchase the maps separately. To download the Harvey map of the Skye trail cost £16. The main advantage of the View Ranger over Satmap is the far better screen definition and hence a much clearer image, indeed indistinguishable from having the map open in front of you.

However, there are disadvantages. Phones are far less robust than a purpose built outdoors device, and more susceptible to damp and damage if dropped. The battery life will be rapidly depleted if using the View Ranger app constantly. Your phone battery needs to be preserved in case of an emergency when you may need it to summon help. So it is not a good idea to run it flat by using it as a navigation aid.

You can take steps to conserve the battery. Turn off all background apps which are often running unseen, and switch to Airplane mode. This will not prevent View Ranger receiving a satellite signal, but it will cut out most other battery-draining activity. If View Ranger is used sparingly with these precautions, and in low power mode, I find I can still have 90% battery on my phone at the end of a day's walking.

So it is a 'belt and braces' approach for me: map, GPS and phone.

BEN DEARG TO PORTREE

I wake early and try to get back to sleep but to no avail, so decide I might as well get up. I enjoy mornings the best. There is a chill in the air and the scenery looks so different. During the daytime, the bright sun has been high in the sky, so there have been no shadows and no depth to the scenery. The heat haze has blurred the distant views and many photographs are disappointing, failing to capture the dramatic scenery.

Early morning view east from below Ben Dearg

But this morning, although the sun is already quite high in the sky, it is sending shafts of sunlight through the clouds creating a vivid scene. The view across to the mainland is breathtaking.

It is completely silent except for the occasional cuckoo which I have heard every day from morning till night. There is no wind, no traffic, no people, no noise, just me and my little tent. I am always surprised how small and insignificant it looks in such majestic surroundings. The joy of wild camping; freedom, solitude and nature. As I stand there feeling at one with the world an eagle glides gently by along the cliff edge close to my tent. It is gone too soon to catch a photograph, but perhaps that is how it should be. A truly magical moment.

The clouds and the chill in the air suggest there may be a change in the weather. Still I can't complain after such glorious dry weather so far. I have my cup of tea and quickly pack up. I am now into a smooth routine and know where things go and how to pack everything away efficiently and in the logical order. Soon I am off and heading towards Ben Dearg, the prospect of which had deterred me from continuing last night.

The official route goes directly towards the steep north face but then diverts to the west along the contour to reach the ridge line before turning sharply back on itself to head up the ridge towards the summit. However, as I approach the foot of the face where the route turns right, I notice a direct route straight ahead which has clearly been used by others, much shorter but also much steeper. I ponder for a few moments whether to go for it, or play it safe and take the more cautious longer route.

Buoyed up mentally by my early morning experience and with fresh legs to carry me physically, I opt for the direct route. It starts getting steeper, but the ground underfoot is firm and with the aid of my poles I push onward and upward. But progressively it gets even steeper and the ground becomes less sure, until I am on an exposed face on scree and loose rock. I am reduced to scrambling and using my hands for extra support. Just below the top I am feeling too exposed, so traverse right to slightly more secure footholds. Eventually I reach safe ground above, and see the summit. I feel elated, though with hindsight it was perhaps foolish.

From hereon to Portree, it is mostly downhill, though the walking is still not easy as the terrain is uneven, scrubby with gorse and heather and boggy in places despite the dry weather. It is not as dramatic or scenic as the northern section of the ridge, but is less physically tiring. Eventually Portree is glimpsed as it dips in and out of view behind the hills. It feels quite an emotional moment. Although I still have three days to go, I have completed the highest and most exposed part of the Trail along the Trotternish Ridge. It is effectively a walk of two halves: the first being high level hill walking and the second lower level roads and paths. I feel a sense of achievement at what I have accomplished so far. I reach a road and it is just a short walk to Torvaig campsite north of Portree. I arrive as hoped about midday so I can have an afternoon to relax and explore the town.

It is an attractive campsite with smooth, green grassy pitches. There is a mix of small tents, touring tents and campervans. The person on reception is friendly and welcoming, as is everyone I have met so far on Skye. I spot some gas cartridges and assume they are for sale, but he invites me to help myself as they have been left by other campers who are flying home so cannot take them. I am delighted as I need to replenish my gas supply.

Once my tent is pitched, I have a shower to freshen up and decide to rinse through a t-shirt and a pair of pants. With the hot weather still prevailing, I am hopeful I can get them dry. Then early afternoon I head downhill into Portree. It is a pretty harbour town, the largest on Skye, bustling with tourists and cars, and with a prosperous feel.

The pretty harbour at Portree

My first task is to find something to eat, and when I spy a fish and chip shop it is an easy decision. Suitably replenished I wander round the town centre where just three days ago I caught the bus to start the Trail. It seems like an eon ago. Three days at home passes just like that, yet when outdoors, busy and active it seems like an eternity. Perhaps

Einstein was right, time is relative.

I buy another gas cylinder just in case, despite the free one from the campsite. I would rather take it home unused (which in the event I did) than run out. No gas equals no hot water and therefore no food and no cup of tea. I also buy some food for tonight and snacks for the next three days. Finally I treat myself to a cup of coffee and a slice of shortcake. It is wonderful how the little pleasures in life grow in importance after a few days walking and wild camping.

The road back up to the campsite from the centre of Portree is quite a trek, so I am glad I did not have to do it carrying my pack, knowing I would just be retracing my steps the following morning. Back at the campsite, I spot the strangest camping arrangement I have ever seen. It is an inflated tent on a roof rack on an ordinary family car, accessed via an aluminium stepladder!

Well, it's different

I fail to see the point. It has none of the benefits of a proper camper van such as a kitchen or toilet; and none of the advantages of a proper tent. You can't stand up in it, barely dress and undress in it, or cook or sit or shelter from the elements. It is just a bed on a roof rack. And if you want to go and sightsee for the day you would have to completely dismantle it. I dread to think how it would cope with high winds or bad weather. Still, live and let live. It provided some amusement for other campers on the site.

I have a pleasant surprise later in the afternoon. A woman approaches and greets me, and it is the German lady who with her Canadian companions so kindly gave me water yesterday morning. We chat for a while about her plans and I thank her again for the water.

The evening is uneventful. I stay at the campsite, have a beer I bought in Portree, read my Kindle, write up my diary and then settle down for the night ready for the next morning.

PORTREE TO LOCH DUBHA

I have three long days ahead of me as I am combining the last four stages into three. I could have walked further yesterday afternoon, but opted to explore Portree and take the opportunity for a bit of rest and relaxation. But now I need to get moving. The stretch from Portree to Sligachan is the section which it was suggested I should miss out as being too boring, but I intend to complete the full Trail so choose not to heed the advice.

From the campsite I return downhill into Portree. The morning is cool as I set out, as the sun still has to warm the air from the overnight chill. As I enter Portree a friendly local lady comments on the size of my pack and chats to me as we walk along together for a short distance. I have found the people on Skye to be so friendly and welcoming.

The path leaves the road a kilometre south of the town and heads to the rocky shore of Portree bay. The next short section skirting along the shore and looking across the salt water marshes is delightful. The evocative smell of sea air and seaweed brings back memories of seaside holidays.

But too soon the path joins a small road and the next 9kms are on tarmac. It is pleasant enough walking, though when cars come along it is necessary to stand aside as the road is too narrow for them to pass in safety. Most drivers give a cheery wave which reinforces the warm impression I have of Skye.

A red post office van overtakes me and stops ahead. I see the postman jump out to empty one of those small, isolated country postboxes perched on a metal pole. It strikes me that at this moment postmen and women will be doing the same all over the country, collecting millions of letters for delivery the next day to anywhere throughout the country, all for a fixed, flat rate fee. A truly remarkable service and one we should value. Well done Royal Mail.

The salt water marshes of Portree Bay

An abundance of bluebells on the road from Portree to Peinachorrain

The roadside verges are lined with an abundance of bluebells for mile after mile. It is a most wonderful sight. In England one has to make a special journey to see bluebell woods, but here they are found all over.

I walk through the small village of Braes with its community hall. The village is famous for The Battle of the Braes, commemorated further along the road by a small memorial. A group of crofters organised a petition for the return of grazing land seized during the Highland clearances, and refused to pay rent until it was granted.

In April 1882 the Sheriff arrived from Portree to serve summonses for eviction, but was forced to retreat when confronted by an angry mob and the summonses were burnt. Warrants were then issued for the arrest of the ringleaders and 40 police were sent from Glasgow to carry out the orders. Arriving at 6am one morning, a pitched battle ensued with many injuries, but eventually the police managed to escape with their prisoners, who were subsequently tried without a jury, found guilty and imprisoned. The newspapers dubbed it The Battle of the Braes.

Memorial to The Battle of the Braes

The unrest spread more widely throughout Skye and public sympathy lay with the crofters. Questions were asked in Parliament and an inquiry was demanded. Eventually, after further confrontations and even the dispatch of a navy gunboat, Prime Minister Gladstone conceded, and in 1886, four years after The Battle of the Braes, the Crofters Act was passed giving every crofter security of tenure.

The final section of the walk along the road is through the pretty hamlet of Balmeanach alongside the sandy bay of the same name. This is a sheltered spot and the houses, gardens, trees and vegetation are reminiscent of a pretty seaside town in England rather than the harsher landscape elsewhere on Skye. It is peaceful, tranquil and beautiful. The day so far has not been as exciting or challenging as the Ridge and has almost all been on tarmac, but it has been pretty and with some interest, so I am glad I have done it; but the next stage to reach Sligachan is indeed worth missing out.

It is some 6kms along the shore of Loch Sligachan on a rough and uneven path requiring careful attention. The destination point of the whitewashed Sligachan Hotel is visible almost from the outset, yet frustratingly seems to get no closer. It is a long and unremitting slog, and by mid-afternoon I am feeling exhausted, but want to make it to the hotel where I plan to stop for something to eat. A French man walking in the other direction stops to ask about the path, the tide and possible camping stops. Even though I am impatient to reach my goal, I help a fellow walker as much as I am able with advice and information.

Slowly the hotel comes into closer focus, but annoyingly there are still streams to cross and the path is unclear, before finally I finally reach the campsite a short distance before the hotel. It looks attractive and I am sorely tempted to stop here for the night, but if I do I know I will not be able to complete the Trail over the next two days and will have to take a bus at some point to get back by Sunday evening. I ask a gardener tending the grounds to take my photo and he chats about the hot, dry weather and my plans, and helpfully points out the path for my next stage. But I am tired and hungry and just want to get into the hotel, so once politeness allows I bid him farewell. I fill my water bottles from the campsite tap and walk the final short distance to reach the hotel.

As I cross the car park, just about to enter the door of the Seamus bar, a French couple stop me and ask if I speak French. In the interests of European harmony I admit I do, and they ask which is the road for Ferrypool. I have never heard of Ferrypool, but keen to be helpful, I ask to look at the guide book they are holding, and discover it is the Fairy Pool they are seeking! I tell them it is on the Glenbrittle road and point out the direction. But they don't seem convinced and as far as I can gather they have already driven this road and not found it. I have done enough for the 'entente cordiale' and really do need to get inside and sit down, so I say goodbye.

Finally, finally at 3.30pm I am inside. It is a large bar and I slump into a chair exhausted. I order fish and chips from the friendly staff behind the bar and a pint of lemonade and lime to slake my thirst. It is wonderful what a bit of food, drink and rest can do. Within half an hour I am re-energised and all thoughts of camping here tonight are banished. So an hour later I step out into the bright sunshine and set off again south along the stunning Glen Sligachan.

After the trials of the morning and early afternoon, this part of the Trail is one of the best. On the right are the majestic Black Cuillin Hills and to the left the Red Cuillins. The obvious path follows the River Sligachan snaking along the Glen and makes for easy walking, rising only gently uphill. After my low point earlier in the afternoon I am now in good spirits. The weather and scenery could not be better.

Glen Sligachan with the Cuillin range in the background

As I walk, I stop to chat to an Italian walker who is heading to Sligachan carrying a large rucksack, and then later a young Australian woman in shorts and t-shirt, with no pack and just carrying a water bottle. This seems incongruous as we are in the middle of Glen Sligachan some distance from any safety and it is late afternoon. Everyone else I have seen is equipped for hill walking with at least a day pack if not a full overnight pack. But she is obviously confident and at home in the outdoors. She tells me she set off from Sligachan at 3pm and has climbed Marsco, a 736m summit, and is now on her way down. After a friendly chat she heads off at speed. She puts my slow and steady plod to shame.

At about 7pm, after 2½ hours walking from Sligachan, I reach the small Loch Dubha slightly below me in the Glen, my planned location for camping tonight. But it is not easy to find a suitable spot. There is plenty of space, but the ground is sloping, stony, uneven and covered in gorse and heather. I dump my rucksack and spend some time searching, walking down towards the Loch and uphill to get a better view of the area. Eventually I decide on a small flat area which will have to do and I quickly pitch my tent. It is a lovely setting and a beautiful evening.

Camping in Glen Sligachan overlooked by the Cuillins

I have soon sorted my gear inside the tent, prepared my evening meal and then get ready to settle in for the night. It is my fifth night and I am well into my routine by now. A mountain biker zooms past shouting a cheery goodnight. One is never quite completely alone.

SAFETY

In 2017 there were 2396 emergency call-outs for Mountain Rescue teams in England and Wales, up from 2074 the previous year. Some of these are unavoidable, but many others are due to ignorance or inexperience. We have all read stories of walkers wearing jeans and with no map getting lost on a hill as the weather turns for the worse. The practical guidance in this book should help to prepare you better for the challenges of walking safely in the hills and reduce the likelihood of you becoming the next statistic.

Of course, walking in the hills always carries a certain risk, even for the most careful or experienced walker. A stumble, a slip, a loose rock or a slippery path and a broken wrist or sprained ankle can happen in an instant. So be prepared and take precautions. As an ex-member of a Mountain Rescue team, I have attended incidents where well-equipped, fit and experienced walkers or climbers have suffered unexpected problems and ended up in difficulties. Don't think it can't happen to you.

As a 69 year-old walking alone on Skye, I was aware that I was placing myself at greater risk than a younger person walking with others who can assist and alert the authorities if necessary. But equally, crossing the road or driving both carry risks and we do them all the time. We cannot wrap ourselves in cotton wool, and discovering our limits is part of the reason why so many people take part in sport or adventures.

However, this does not mean you should be the one who sets off wearing jeans, without a map or waterproofs and without checking the weather forecast. There is a difference between adventure and foolhardiness; the latter places both you and the rescue services at risk. So what are the sensible precautions to minimise risk and maximise your chances of survival if stuck overnight on the hills?

Know and accept your limitations of fitness, experience, confidence and health. Plan a trip that may stretch and challenge you, but not overwhelm you. Prepare for it by improving your level of fitness and strength, so if you need to press on later and longer than planned to find an overnight spot, you have something in reserve.

As already detailed under the navigation section, take a map and compass and know how to use them. I have no problem with electronic aids, but they can fail. Take a fully charged mobile phone, and save its battery in case you need it for an emergency, don't waste it posting to Facebook. If you must, save that for when you are in the pub and can plug in to recharge.

If you need to call for help it is possible to send an emergency message by text, but you must register before you can use this service. Do it before you depart, don't wait until you are in need. It is simple, just text 'register' to 999 and follow the instructions. Once registered you can call for emergency help by text.

This has a number of advantages over making a voice call. The most crucial is that if you have a poor signal, a text needs only a moment to send, whereas a voice call may get cut off before you can even talk to an operator. Also, if it is windy or noisy you do not have any problems with being unable to hear or be heard. In your text say you need mountain rescue (assuming you are in an isolated location) and give details of who, what and where. Even if your phone is showing no signal, try sending a text, as calls to 999 will connect to any available network, not just your own. However, the emergency services cannot call you back on a network that is not your own, so make sure you include full and accurate information in your message.

For location, a grid reference is by far the most helpful if on the hills, as it can be hard to give an accurate description. So you must know how to obtain a grid reference from a map, which of course requires you to know where you are on the map. But as with navigation, electronic aids are often more convenient. Both Satmap and the View Ranger app will give your location as a grid reference; or you can download the OS Locate app for free which is a fast and highly accurate means of pinpointing your exact location. It does not rely on a phone signal but uses the inbuilt GPS system. However, electronic aids can fail, so make sure you know how to get a map reference from a map.

If you are in contact with Mountain Rescue they can locate you using SARLOC. The rescue team will send you an SMS text message with a link to a webpage. When you click on this link it opens a page in your phone's browser which identifies your location. This data is then sent automatically over the internet to the Mountain Rescue team base. Even if you are moving, it will track you in real time.

There is also a safety app called Uepaa! which you can download for free on your phone. It connects you to a world-wide safety network via a 24/7 Emergency Centre, and also to any users of the app nearby. You can trigger an alert for help if you are in difficulties, and a location engine logs your last known position. Your personal emergency contacts will also be notified. I have never had to use it so cannot vouch for its success, but it is free, so worth downloading.

The top of the range safety device is a Personal Locator Beacon. This is a small portable transmitter that when activated sends out a personalised emergency distress signal via satellites and ground stations. The battery life is designed to continue sending out the signal for at least 24 hours. The signal will identify you and your location, and alert the local first responder emergency services wherever you are. The units are about the size of a wallet, weigh up to 1kgm and cost around £150-£300. I don't carry one, but if you are travelling alone in remote areas without phone signal coverage, then they give peace of mind to both you and your relatives.

You must leave details of your planned route (and any possible detours) with someone who can alert the rescue services if you don't return. I leave my route and planned overnight stops with my wife, but make her aware that I may not be able to make contact on a regular basis as phone reception is often poor or non-existent in remote areas, so not to panic if she doesn't hear from me.

For this trip, as I was staying at the same B&B at the start and at the end of my trip, I left my route plan with the owners, and also the phone number to contact my wife. I explained if I didn't return as planned they should telephone the rescue services, and my wife to ascertain when and where I had last made contact. This would reduce the search area down to the point from my last known contact to the finish, almost certainly less than the whole 128kms of the Skye trail.

Plan possible escape routes from exposed situations in case the weather turns nasty or you find yourself exhausted. On the Skye Trail the Trotternish ridge is the most exposed. Unfortunately, there are no obvious escape routes after the Uig to Staffin road until you get to The Storr some 21kms later. On the rest of the route there are possibilities to abandon the walk and take a bus at various points, and in any case the route is not so high or exposed, so the need for an escape is less pressing.

Take sufficient warm clothing, waterproof clothing, food and water to cope with a change in the weather for the worse and the possibility, especially if injured, of having to stay put until help arrives. I carry a 'survival bag', a bright orange, heavy-duty plastic 'bivvy' bag, capable of keeping out wind and rain, and large enough to get inside with a sleeping bag. If I am carrying a tent, I do not take a casualty shelter - a sort of lightweight tent without any poles - which can be used to provide protection by getting inside and sitting on the edges to keep it in place. If necessary the flysheet of my tent can serve much the same purpose. However, if travelling without a tent, then a casualty shelter is a wise precaution.

Check the weather forecast, but don't rely on it; especially in Scotland where the old adage of 'four seasons in one day' is especially applicable.

The weather can suddenly turn for the worse with hail and wind sweeping in on a previously warm and sunny day. Skye is as far north as Alaska, Hudson Bay, southern Sweden and southern Siberia; and further north than Moscow. The only reason it is typically spared the extreme weather experienced in these places is thanks to the warming waters of the Gulf Stream. But don't let this lull you into a false sense of security; it can be vicious.

Carry a whistle and a torch. The recognised distress signal is six blasts or flashes repeated at one minute intervals. The reply if rescue services hear you is three blasts. Keep whistling or flashing even if you know help is at hand, to assist the rescuers locate you as easily and quickly as possible.

Finally, a first aid kit is essential, though how extensive is a matter of judgement. Certainly you need plasters, stretch bandage, wound dressing, zinc tape, antiseptic wipes and antiseptic cream. A more comprehensive (but heavier) kit might also include gauze padding, eye pad, safety pins, triangular bandage, painkillers, aspirin (for heart attack not pain relief), glucose tablets (for hypoglycaemia), eye wash, scissors, tweezers, disposable gloves and a first aid manual. Of course, you will also need any medicines that you have been prescribed, an inhaler if you have asthma, an EpiPen if you have allergies and GTN spray if you have angina. If you have concerns about your health, you should consult your GP before you depart.

If you follow all this advice you are less likely to become a statistic and if mishap befalls you, much more likely to be equipped to survive until help arrives. All Mountain Rescue team members are volunteers, so consider making a donation; you never know when you might need them.

LOCH DUBHA TO LOCH SLAPIN

It rained during the night, the first significant rain I have had this week. For Scotland I have been so lucky. I spot the outline of a dark shape on the outer side of my inner tent door!. Investigation reveals a large slug which has climbed up there during the night. I am pleased the door was zipped shut as I would not have welcomed it inside the tent in the night. I gently return it to the grass outside, where I am sure it will be much happier. I certainly am.

When I emerge I realise the rain sounds much worse inside than in reality is the case. It is the same with wind. Stormy gusts inside turn out to be a mild breeze when one emerges. The tent has resisted the rain admirably. The water is beading in large droplets on the outside and running down to the ground. The damp conditions necessitate packing up as much as possible inside the tent, for the first time. It is only a small one-person tent, so stuffing my sleeping bag and roll mat and pillow into their respective stuff sacs is a struggle in such a cramped space. Luckily I do not need to try and boil up water inside the tent, as the rain is now almost stopped, so I can enjoy my cup of tea outside. However, it remains dull and grey.

Three walkers arrive from the south heading towards Sligachan. They had camped a short way further along the glen and are now heading for home. They are in a cheery mood and stop for a chat. Everyone on the Trail is friendly, and there is a bond of camaraderie amongst those wild camping along the route, easily identified by their large packs. One feels a sense of pride over day-walkers, and certainly over tourists just strolling from a car park.

I pack up and continue my walk south along Glen Sligachan with towering mountains on both sides. It is a truly magnificent part of the trail. It is not busy, but I meet occasional other walkers, most of them from overseas. Along the Trail I have met and chatted with people from France, Germany, Italy, Canada, Poland and Australia. They are drawn by the attraction of the scenery and also Scotland's tolerant attitude towards wild camping. Long may it last.

Early morning shot of the misty Cuillins

After a couple of hours walking a view of Camasunary Bay appears ahead. The path descends to an area of flat coastal grass leading down towards the shore. A whitewashed private house stands next to the now derelict original bothy, but a smart new one built in 2014 is to be found about a kilometre further along the shore. I head inside and find two walkers engrossed in completing a multi-piece jigsaw they had started the previous night and cannot bring themselves to leave until it is completed.

The bothy can sleep up to fifteen people and the jigsaw puzzlers tell me seven had been there last night. I prefer greater solitude. But outside, the bay would be a superb wild camping spot. Unfortunately my timetable did not allow for an overnight here, but if ever I return it will be on my list.

From here onwards the walking becomes harder. The path follows the shore for a while and then ascends to continue along the cliff face above the rocky shoreline below. The guide book advises extreme care on this 'vertiginous' path. I would strongly endorse this. The narrow path clings to the side of the cliff with often little between me and a near vertical drop that would certainly result in serious injury and probably worse. In places it is so eroded I am stepping across open gaps with nothing but fresh air below me. I cannot believe it will last as a viable path much longer without significant maintenance. Heavy rainfall will erode the muddy parts further until it surely becomes impassable. Luckily I am walking on a day with little wind and no rain. In slippery or blustery conditions beware.

Halfway along it descends to the shoreline and a bay at the outflow of Glen Scaladal. This would also make a lovely wild camping spot. However, one is afforded only a short respite before the path rises again along the cliff face for another perilous stage. As well as being exposed it is undulating, uneven and in places overgrown with vegetation.

View down to the harbour at Elgol

By mid-afternoon I am feeling exhausted and wondering if I should stop at Elgol the next village, rather than continue to my planned overnight stop. I have noticed this pattern to the days as I walk. I feel strong for the first six hours or so and make good progress, but then start to flag during the afternoon. But I have found rest, food and drink work their magic and I gain a second wind and have been able to walk for another few hours till early evening. Fortunately, today fits this established pattern. The tiny fishing port of Elgol comes into view, but it takes an age to reach, as my progress along this difficult path is painfully slow.

The harbour is a popular tourist spot for boat trips to the isles of Rum, Canna, Eigg and Soay as well as Loch Coruisk. After a day of walking in near solitude, it makes a marked contrast to find it busy with visitors. I head into the small village shop and café and sink onto a chair, relieved to be free of the weight of my pack and able to give my legs a rest. There is no hot food, so it is a cup of tea, egg mayo roll and lemon drizzle cake. The lady serving is friendly, as everyone has been, and refills my water bottles.

She tells me the Blue Cabin café at Torrin is completely closed at the moment. Luckily, I had not planned on eating there as I will arrive tomorrow on a Sunday morning when it would normally have been closed anyway, but for the moment it is closed permanently. Apparently the owner sold it and then the sale fell through. So at the time of writing it awaits a new owner. Check on the website if you are planning on walking the Trail and hoping to stop here for food.

Head to head with a magnificent beast

Rest and sustenance do the trick, and I set off with a renewed spring in my step, which I need as I still have some 12kms to my planned overnight spot slightly before Torrin. Fortunately, the walking is much easier underfoot than earlier, as it is now mostly road or track. But it starts with a long uphill stretch across the southern peninsula to reach the eastern coastline before turning north. I have reached the southern extremity of the trail from my northern starting point at Rubha Hunish.

The grassy track passes through woodland with an abundance of the most beautiful bluebells, and cuckoos sounding their call all the time. It is a change from the more open and bare landscape I have generally been walking through. As I leave the woods and follow the track, I come face to face with a large longhorn Highland bull. He is standing in the middle of the path and not looking to move. He shows little interest in me as I skirt cautiously around him and continue on my way.

Eventually the path heads down to the shore at the southern end of Loch Slapin and joins a minor road leading past Kilmarie House, once owned by Ian Anderson, the lead singer and flautist of the early seventies rock band Jethro Tull. He also owned the Strathaird Estate and established a successful fish farming business employing hundreds of local people. He sold the estate to the John Muir Trust in 1994.

Kilmarie House once owned by Ian Anderson of Jethro Tull

The Trail continues along a road and then heads on a path uphill alongside Forestry Commission land to pass the abandoned village of Keppoch, cleared of 44 families in 1852, many sent to Australia, as part of the infamous Highland Clearances.

The final 3kms seem a long downhill slog. I am feeling tired, it has started to rain and it is getting late. Eventually I arrive at the northern tip of Loch Slapin, my destination for the night. I spy a group of tents with a campfire, so decide to camp slightly further along in case of any noise. Fortunately there are plenty of nice spots along the shore so I put down my pack at the first one I find. It is 8pm. Soon the tent is up, my evening meal (sweet and sour pork with rice) is rehydrated and eaten and I am beginning to recover. It was an 11 hour day of walking with just a one hour break at Elgol. The light rain is still falling and the midges are out, so it is time to get some sleep.

LOCH SLAPIN TO BROADFORD

It was raining overnight and is continuing this morning, though thankfully not heavily. I cannot complain, as I have enjoyed wonderful weather for almost all of my trip, and even when it has rained it has only ever been drizzle. I am looking forward to my final day and sleeping in a comfortable bed tonight and enjoying a beer. But before that I have 23kms of walking.

Camping by Loch Slapin under a glowering sky

The tent is soon packed away, but the midges are out in force for the first time and I have to don my midge net as I pack my sack and eat my breakfast. I set off feeling fit and strong. I have felt better each day rather than getting tired or stiff as the week has progressed. Only the mid-afternoon slump has been a challenge.

I walk around the northern tip of Loch Slapin and head towards the tiny hamlet of Torrin. The Blue Cabin Café is indeed closed as I was warned yesterday by the lady at Elgol. It is in a lovely setting and will make a good little business for someone. The weather is brightening up and the rain has stopped as I leave Torrin and pass the local quarry which has been extracting limestone and marble since the 18th century. Once round the quarry, the road leads to the coast and then heads south on an uphill track towards Suisnish.

I meet a young couple with climbing gear and chat with them for a short distance, but they are walking more quickly than me so they move on ahead. My next meeting is with a Polish walker who is on the first day of the Trail heading in the opposite direction. He has ambitious plans, but is young and fit so will no doubt be fine.

The way ahead is blocked

And now we return to the encounter introduced in the Prologue. I round a corner and am faced by six cows, five calves and a bull standing across my path. Cows and calves is a dangerous combination, but I cannot just stand here and wait. As I slowly approach, they amble gently ahead of me not looking upset or worried, but always moving on as I approach. So long as they continue walking ahead of me I am not overly concerned.

But when a couple appear ahead over the brow of the hill the whole mood changes. They stop eating, turn to look behind at me and then ahead at the new arrivals. They are feeling trapped and wanting to escape. I am in the firing line being downhill from them. I stop, as do the couple ahead of me. Stalemate.

I edge gently off the path sideways up the hill. As soon as their escape route is clear they stampede downhill through where I had been standing. I hear the snorting of the bull pass close behind me! The danger is averted.

The couple resume their downhill walk and I continue uphill; we stop to talk. They are also on their first day of the Trail. It feels good being on my last day crossing over with people on their first. They ask for advice on camping spots and I suggest Loch Slapin, otherwise there is not a lot all the way to Elgol, nor for some distance afterwards. Shortly afterwards, I arrive at the abandoned village of Suisnish, another victim of the clearances in 1853. Here the path turns east following the coast of Loch Eishort along the cliff top.

On the cliff top path before the descent to the shore

I have not seen more than a handful of people all day, but I now hear a babble of voices ahead of me and spy a group of perhaps 30 people standing on a promontory at the cliff edge. When I reach them I ask if this is a 'Gathering of the Clans', and am met with a blank stare. I then discover they are French, so my friendly jocular greeting fell on stony ground. I retrieve Anglo-French relations by speaking in French and asking one of them to take my photo.

The path descends steeply from this point and yet more walkers are still puffing their way up the path, not looking the fittest. I discern it is an organised group on a day walk. I am pleased to move on and return to peace and solitude. I have my lunch on the stony beach below, rehydrating a cheesy pasta sachet and having a cup of coffee. I am looking forward to proper food this evening.

So the final leg begins, along the rocky shore and then climbing steadily uphill to arrive at Boreraig, yet another village cleared and burnt by Lord MacDonald's men to make way for sheep farming. The census of 1851 records 120 men, women and children living in 22 households. All were cleared in 1853, many taking the option to emigrate to Australia. It lies in a fertile glen but has a melancholy air because of its sad history.

Ruined house in the village of Boreraig

The path turns north after Boreraig heading towards Broadford, but still uphill. I am feeling impatient to get to the end now, but it is some 8kms to go. I arrive at the highest point on this final stretch and begin the last descent; it is all downhill from here. My customary afternoon dip in energy arrives, but I do not want to take a long break to recharge my batteries, I just want to get finished; so I press on at speed.

The path passes the remains of an old marble quarry and follows the route of the Marble Line, a railway built in 1907 to transport the quarried marble to Broadford. But the quarry closed in 1912 and the line is now a popular walking route. The end point comes into sight as the path skirts along the contours of Ben Suardal, and finally I arrive at the Broadford Hotel on the outskirts of the town. It is another kilometre to my B&B, which seems the longest on the whole Trail. I am so nearly there but have to walk along the High Street, past the ugly Co-op store and uphill to the Carrick, arriving at 5.30pm.

As I approach the entrance, Piet emerges applauding me and shakes my hand; how welcoming. I am exhausted and elated in equal measure. I dump my rucksack straight into the boot of my vehicle and swap it for the bag with my change of clean clothes. I head upstairs for a cup of tea followed by a hot bath to soak away the dirt and relax my muscles. Apart from being tired, I am feeling in excellent shape; no injuries, no aches or pains, no accidents. A successful trip.

After my bath I open a bottle of beer I had left in my bag, and with my energy restored I head out into Broadford to eat. Piet kindly offers to give me a lift but I say it is not necessary. I head to the Dunollie Hotel and into the bar, not the restaurant. I want to be able to relax, eat and drink at my own pace, check my phone for messages and look at my photos. I order a pint and steak and chips, both of which taste delicious. It is a wonderful feeling to have pushed myself hard, had a great experience and now be back safe and sound in civilisation.

I head back to the Carrick and a proper bed for the first time in a week. I sleep well.

EPILOGUE

The journey back home was uneventful, and with my gear unpacked, cleaned and laid out to dry I had a chance over subsequent days to reflect on my trip. It was exactly what I had hoped for: challenging, remote and with wild camping in beautiful scenery.

The Trotternish ridge was tough, and the lack of water would have been problematic but for the kindness of fellow walkers giving me two litres. I certainly would recommend splitting the Ridge into two stages rather than attempting to walk from Flodigarry to The Storr in one day as suggested in the Guide book. I made up the extra day I spent on the Ridge by completing the final four stages in three. With hindsight, I should just have added a day to the trip and taken it at a more leisurely pace.

The distances over the final three days were not unreasonable, ranging from 22 to 26.5kms, but some of the walking was difficult because of the terrain, and this slowed my speed, meaning I was walking till 8pm one evening. The section from Peinachorrain to Sligachan was rocky and uneven along the shores of Loch Sligachan; the section from Camasunary to Elgol was on a narrow, exposed and uneven cliff edge path which similarly made for very slow progress.

Both of these tedious sections arrived as I hit my early afternoon dip in energy, further reducing my rate of progress. Fortunately, in both cases food, drink and a rest restored my energy and I was able to continue for another three or four hours and walk a further 7 and 14.5kms. But it would have been more enjoyable to take things at a more relaxed pace, set camp earlier and feel less tired.

I was pleased with my careful planning, even though I revised my plan on the first day having accepted a lift to Portree which enabled me to catch an earlier bus to the start, and being advised that Rubha Hunish bothy gets crowded. My ability to make this spontaneous change of plan whilst travelling in the bus was only possible because I had knowledge of the route, the distance and time to Flodigarry and the availability of camping when I arrived there.

I was mistaken in the availability of water on the Ridge. This was partly because the weather was unseasonably hot and the ground was baked dry; and the also because advice received from posts on Facebook sites was overly optimistic. I would advise anyone planning to walk the length of the Ridge to take sufficient water to get from the Uig road crossing to The Storr without expecting to resupply.

By contrast, my food planning worked perfectly. I finished with one spare meal which was my reserve, and I restocked as planned with snacks in Portree. I was not planning on eating at the Blue Cabin café, which was fortunate as it was completely closed.

My accommodation was an excellent choice. I could leave my vehicle for the week whilst I walked, the bedroom and breakfast were excellent and the owners friendly and helpful. The offer of transport for my pack to meet up with me at the bus station on the first day was much appreciated.

There were some items of kit I did not use, but that is not the same as saying they were not necessary. Kit that never came out was overtrousers, gaiters, thermal top and long johns, gilet, gloves, tick removal tweezers, First Aid kit, Compeed plasters, 'bivvy' bag and torch. But I would not have left any of these behind. I was fortunate with the weather and thankfully avoided injuries and blisters; but one never knows.

My Satmap Active 10 performed perfectly and proved its value, though I did also refer to my Harvey's map at intervals to review my progress. There is no path for much of the Trail, and in bad weather or poor visibility there are places where extreme care would be needed. Fortunately, I had no problem being able to see my way at all times. My phone battery lasted the whole week, but I only switched it on once a day, as did my Sony Cybershot camera which took all the pictures in this book.

People in Skye and those I met on the Trail were universally friendly and helpful. The scenery as everyone knows is wonderful, but it can still take the breath away. For me Glen Sligachan was the most stunning part of the trail with the Black and Red Cuillin mountains to right and left. Camasunary bay was beautiful and would have made a perfect wild camping spot.

So, a successful trip with near perfect weather, Skye looking at its best and midges not at their worst. Here's to the next adventure.

ABOUT THE AUTHOR

The author is a 69 year old retired psychologist, a keen walker, camper and climber, and a past member of a Mountain Rescue Team. He has walked the West Highland Way with his son, the Coast to Coast footpath, the Dales Way and the East Highland Way. In 2015 he climbed Kilimanjaro with his daughter, and in 2017 trekked in Nepal visiting Everest Base Camp, crossing three high passes and reaching two summits. He is married with two children and three grandchildren. He has lived near Bolton since 1989. This is his second book.

He can be contacted at david.crawford345@gmail.com.

46766706R00056

Printed in Poland
by Amazon Fulfillment
Poland Sp. z o.o., Wrocław